RSD: Living, Laughing and Loving with Rejection Sensitive Dysphoria

Jack Patrick

Published by Boomer Publishing, 2025.

RSD: LIVING, LAUGHING AND LOVING WITH REJECTION SENSITIVE DYSPHORIA

First edition. November 1, 2025.

ISBN: 978-1067068233

Written by Jack Patrick.

Table of Contents

For anyone who has ever wondered why small things hurt so much.

RSD: Living, Laughing and Loving with Rejection Sensitivity Dysphoria

Jack Patrick

Table of Contents

Introduction

Welcome to this guide to Rejection Sensitive Dysphoria or, as it's more commonly known, RSD.

We all care what others think of us. That's human. Our brains are wired to connect, to belong, to be seen and accepted. But for some people, that sensitivity to approval and rejection doesn't just shape their social lives. It defines them. It governs every interaction, controls every risk, and colours every success or failure with a powerful emotional charge that can be hard to explain to others.

This is where Rejection Sensitive Dysphoria enters the picture.

Chapter by chapter we're going to look at what RSD feels like and what it does to those who have it, as well as the effect it has on those who live and work alongside them: parents, partners, friends, teachers, therapists, colleagues, and professionals of all kinds.

While RSD itself is complicated, my purpose here is quite simple: to explain what it is and to try to help those who are directly or indirectly affected by it.

Hopefully, after reading this, you'll have:

- A clearer understanding of what RSD is (and what it is not)
- A sense of where it shows up in life, work, love, and learning
- Language to explain it to others, without having to apologise for yourself or someone close to you
- Acquired practical tools that feel realistic

This book is structured to be readable and useful. It's not a textbook. It's not a clinical manual. It's something you can sit down with, dip into, or share. We'll begin with the fundamentals: what RSD is, how it relates to other neurodivergent traits, and what it looks like in everyday life. From there, we'll move into deeper waters: relationships, identity, parenting, work, therapy, social life. We'll explore the internal experience of RSD, as well as the misunderstandings that surround it.

Later on, there's a dedicated section for the people around those with RSD. If you've picked this up because you care about someone who struggles in any way with RSD, there's a place here for you too.

You'll also find real-world searches scattered throughout; the things that people are actually typing into Google late at night. I've drawn from forums, blogs, and anonymous posts to reflect the raw honesty and reality of those navigating these experiences. Some of these are heartbreaking. Some are wry and self-aware. Some you'll perhaps recognise as the type of things you've been searching for yourself. Either way, all of them speak to the need for a clearer, kinder conversation.

There's a glossary at the front of the book and an FAQ at the end. I've tried to avoid clinical jargon wherever possible, but RSD exists in a space where psychology, neurodivergence, education, and lived experience all collide. Some terminology is unavoidable, but I've tried to make it as easy as possible.

There is also a list of global organisations and references for further reading, and a short section for personal notes if you'd like to reflect on what you've read.

So, wherever you're starting from, welcome. Let's begin.

Glossary

A

ADHD (Attention-Deficit/Hyperactivity Disorder)

A neurodevelopmental condition that affects focus, impulse control, and emotional regulation. RSD is very common in people with ADHD, though not exclusive to it.

Anterior Cingulate Cortex (ACC)

A part of the brain that processes both physical and social pain. It often lights up strongly during rejection, which helps explain why rejection "hurts" so much.

Anxiety

A state of worry or fear that can be mild or overwhelming. RSD often overlaps with anxiety but is not the same thing.

Autism (Autism Spectrum Condition)

A neurodevelopmental condition affecting communication, sensory processing, and social interaction. Many autistic people also experience rejection sensitivity.

B

Behavioural Therapy

Therapies that focus on identifying and changing unhelpful behaviours. Often adapted to help with RSD triggers.

Biology of RSD

Refers to the way brain circuits and chemicals (like dopamine and norepinephrine) amplify sensitivity to rejection. It shows that RSD is rooted in neurology, not "weakness."

Breakups

Romantic or friendship breakups are especially painful in RSD because they combine real loss with the deep fear of abandonment.

C

CBT (Cognitive Behavioural Therapy)

A form of talk therapy that teaches people to challenge negative thoughts. Adapted for RSD, it focuses on reframing assumptions about rejection.

Compassion-Focused Therapy

A therapy that helps people replace harsh self-criticism with kindness toward themselves. Effective for easing the shame linked to RSD.

Coping Strategies

Practical tools for managing distress, like grounding exercises, journaling, or asking for reassurance in safe ways.

Criticism

Feedback that is often perceived as devastating in RSD. Even small comments may feel like proof of unworthiness.

D

Diagnosis

The process of identifying a condition. RSD is not listed in official manuals yet, so diagnosis relies on clinical judgment and self-report.

Disability

In some cases, RSD can be disabling if it significantly disrupts work, education, or daily life. Disability accommodations vary by country.

Dopamine

A neurotransmitter (brain chemical) involved in reward and motivation. Thought to play a role in rejection sensitivity, especially in ADHD.

E

Empathy

The ability to sense and share another's emotions. Often heightened in people with RSD.

Executive Function

Mental processes like planning, organising, and self-control. Often impaired in ADHD and linked to difficulties regulating emotions.

Exclusion

Being left out of a group, event, or activity. For people with RSD, exclusion often feels devastating.

F

FMRI (Functional Magnetic Resonance Imaging)

A brain scan that shows which regions activate during certain tasks. Has been used to demonstrate overlap between physical pain and social pain.

Family Support

The role of family in offering consistency, reassurance, and patience for people with RSD.

Feedback

Input or evaluation given to someone. Even constructive feedback can trigger RSD if not delivered with care.

G

Genetics

The study of inherited traits. Early research suggests rejection sensitivity may have heritable components.

Grief

The sadness of loss. For those with RSD, grief may carry an added layer of feeling abandoned or rejected.

H

Hope

The realistic belief that sensitivity can be managed, improved, and lived with - not erased but balanced.

Hypervigilance

Being constantly on alert for signs of rejection or criticism. Common in RSD.

I

Identity

A person's sense of who they are. RSD can distort identity by making rejection feel like proof of worthlessness.

Isolation

Withdrawing from people to avoid rejection. Feels safer in the moment but often worsens shame.

J

Jealousy

Feelings of fear about being replaced or excluded. In RSD, jealousy is often tied to deep insecurity.

Judgment

Perceived evaluation from others. Even neutral looks or comments may be interpreted as judgment in RSD.

K

Kindness

Small gestures that counterbalance RSD's harsh inner critic. Consistency and care from others are especially powerful.

L

Labels

Words used to describe conditions. Labels like RSD can bring clarity but should not limit identity.

Love

Romantic relationships may feel both intense and fragile with RSD, but can thrive with patience and open communication.

M

Medication

Drugs that may help regulate emotional surges. None are designed specifically for RSD, but some used for ADHD or mood disorders can help.

Mindfulness

Practices that bring attention to the present moment. Helps people observe rejection triggers without being consumed by them.

N

Neurodivergent

An umbrella term for people whose brains process differently, such as those with ADHD or autism. RSD is often part of neurodivergence.

Neurotransmitters

Chemicals that send signals in the brain. Dopamine, norepinephrine, and serotonin are involved in rejection sensitivity.

O

Overreaction

A common accusation against people with RSD. The reaction may look exaggerated but is a genuine neurological surge.

Optimism

The ability to focus on possibilities and hope. Can be cultivated even with RSD.

P

Pacing

A self-management strategy where people conserve energy by balancing activity and rest. Helpful for preventing emotional overload.

Perfectionism

The drive to appear flawless to avoid criticism or rejection. Exhausting but common in RSD.

Prefrontal Cortex

The brain's decision-making hub. Important in regulating emotional responses, often strained in RSD.

PTSD (Post-Traumatic Stress Disorder)

A mental health condition caused by trauma. Shares features with RSD but is a separate condition.

Q

Questionnaires

Tools used in research to measure rejection sensitivity. They are not diagnostic but can highlight patterns.

R

Rejection Sensitivity

The tendency to expect and overreact to rejection. Exists on a spectrum in the general population.

RSD (Rejection Sensitive Dysphoria)

An extreme form of rejection sensitivity where criticism, exclusion, or failure triggers intense emotional pain, often equal to physical pain. Not an official diagnosis yet, but widely recognised by clinicians and patients.

Resilience

The ability to recover from setbacks. Can be cultivated through therapy, community, and values-based living.

Rumination

Repetitive replaying of painful events. A hallmark of RSD.

S

Self-Compassion

Treating oneself with kindness instead of harsh judgment. A powerful antidote to RSD shame.

Serotonin

A brain chemical that regulates mood. Imbalances may heighten sensitivity to rejection.

Shame

The painful belief that one is unworthy. Central in many RSD episodes.

Social Pain

The brain's response to rejection or exclusion. Shown in research to overlap with physical pain circuits.

Spoons (Spoon Theory)

A metaphor used by people with chronic conditions to describe limited energy. RSD flare-ups can "use up spoons," leaving little capacity for other tasks.

Stigma

Negative attitudes toward a condition. People with RSD may be stigmatised as "too sensitive" or "weak."

T

Trauma

A deeply distressing experience. Trauma can worsen rejection sensitivity but is distinct from RSD.

Triggers

Events or cues that spark a strong rejection-sensitive response, such as criticism, silence, or exclusion.

U

Unpredictability

The tendency for small events to cause disproportionately large reactions in RSD.

V

Validation

Acknowledgment that feelings are real and understandable. Essential in supporting someone with RSD.

Values

Guiding principles like kindness or honesty. Anchoring life in values helps people live beyond RSD.

W

Withdrawal

Pulling away from relationships after perceived rejection. A protective instinct that can reinforce shame if prolonged.

Worth

Self-worth is often fragile in RSD, easily tied to others' opinions. Strengthening internal sources of worth is a major therapeutic goal.

Z

Zebra Diagnoses

A phrase used in medicine for rare or overlooked conditions. Sometimes applied by patients who feel their RSD was missed or misunderstood for years.

Chap 1: What Is Rejection Sensitive Dysphoria?

Understanding the Term Beyond the Words

Rejection Sensitive Dysphoria, often abbreviated as RSD, is one of those terms that, once heard, can land with an uncanny sense of recognition. It sounds clinical. It sounds abstract. But for those who live with it, whether they've known the label for years or just stumbled across it, the experience is far from theoretical.

Let's begin plainly. RSD is a condition where rejection, criticism, or even the perceived possibility of either feels emotionally devastating. Not disappointing. Not awkward. Crushing. The intensity of the reaction is what sets it apart. A minor slight or comment that would barely register for one person can ignite a storm of shame, fury, despair, or withdrawal in another. And unlike fleeting mood swings, the emotional waves triggered by RSD can feel immediate, overwhelming, and, in the moment, all-consuming.

People who experience RSD often describe a kind of internal collapse. A breath catches. The gut drops. The mind spirals. Suddenly the room feels unfamiliar, the people in it unreachable. In that moment, nothing feels safe. No relationship feels secure. Trust shatters with startling ease. And even when, later, perspective returns, the pain can still linger—raw and confusing.

RSD Is Not a Personality Flaw

Let's be very clear from the start. This is not about being overly dramatic. It is not about lacking resilience or being "too sensitive." RSD is not a character defect. It is not the fault of a person for feeling too deeply or reacting too strongly. And it certainly is not something people choose to feel.

For many, RSD has roots in neurodivergence, particularly in ADHD and autism, which we'll explore in depth in the next chapter. It is often part of a broader picture of how a person experiences the world: with heightened sensitivity to social dynamics, deep concern about belonging, and an unusually powerful emotional memory. But RSD can also appear in people who don't carry those labels. It can emerge in the aftermath of trauma, long-term invalidation, or early attachment wounds. It can evolve quietly, shaped by years of trying, and failing, to meet impossible standards or navigate unstable relationships.

Whatever the path, the outcome often looks the same: someone who feels like they are "too much" or "not enough," bouncing between trying to be invisible and desperate to be understood.

If that sounds dramatic, that's because RSD is dramatic internally, although it often doesn't look that way on the outside. Many people with RSD become masters of concealment. They mask. They deflect. They make jokes at their own expense before someone else gets the chance. They overachieve, over-apologise, over-explain. Or they disengage entirely, pretending not to care while quietly imploding.

Common Misconceptions

One of the reasons RSD is so often misunderstood is that it mimics other issues. It can look like low self-esteem, but many people with RSD feel confident in their abilities, right up until that moment of perceived rejection. It can look like social anxiety, but the fear is often not about social performance; it's about being liked, accepted, or included. It can even be mistaken for mood disorders, because the emotional swings are so sharp. But RSD reactions are almost always event-triggered, and the emotional fallout tends to resolve as suddenly as it began.

Another common mistake is assuming that people with RSD are "thin-skinned" or can't take feedback. That's not quite right either. In fact, many people with RSD want feedback. They want to improve, connect, and be better. But the delivery matters. A casual remark or unkind tone can hit like a verdict. Even well-meaning advice can be internalised as condemnation. And once that interpretation sets in, it becomes very difficult to undo. The damage, emotionally speaking, is already done.

Real-Life Examples

Let's look at a few examples. These aren't diagnoses. They are sketches; realistic, familiar situations that capture the emotional landscape of RSD.

Case 1: The Missed Text

Sam is in a group chat with a few close friends. Over the weekend, they make plans to meet up, but Sam's suggestion is ignored. Then someone else suggests a similar plan and suddenly everyone is keen. Sam doesn't say anything, but his stomach sinks. He tells himself it doesn't matter. But he stops replying. Later, when one friend checks in, Sam brushes it off. Says he was just busy. But the truth is, he spent the day spiralling, convinced they don't really like him, that he's only tolerated, that he's easy to leave out.

Case 2: The Annual Review

Maria works hard, rarely misses a deadline, and often takes on more than her share. In her annual performance review, her manager praises her work but casually mentions that she "sometimes seems a little intense in meetings." That one line reverberates like a siren. Maria fixates on it for weeks. She replays every meeting in her head, starts holding back in discussions, and avoids speaking up. She tells herself she's being silly, but the self-doubt has lodged deep. It wasn't just a bit of feedback, it felt like she was flawed.

Case 3: The Partner's Sigh

David and his boyfriend are watching TV. David mentions a new project he's excited about and his boyfriend sighs, glancing at his phone. That's all. A sigh. But David's heart races. He feels a sudden urge to apologise, to explain, to backtrack. He's sure he's annoyed him. That he's boring. That the relationship is doomed. He doesn't say any of this. But he goes quiet. Withdraws. Later, he'll pretend nothing happened. But something did. Inside.

These vignettes might sound small. But in the world of RSD, small things aren't small. They are loaded, explosive, sometimes paralysing.

Why It Matters

The cost of living with untreated or misunderstood RSD is not limited to awkward moments. Over time, these experiences can calcify into deep shame, social avoidance, burnout, or chronic self-doubt. Relationships become minefields. Careers stall. Creative ambition dies on the vine. And because the pain feels invisible to others or, even worse, dismissed it breeds isolation.

People with RSD often begin to expect rejection before it happens. They pre-empt it. They sabotage connections. They abandon relationships before they can be abandoned. Some overcorrect, becoming perfectionistic, hyper-vigilant, desperate to please. Others disengage, keeping everyone at arm's length. And still others oscillate between both poles, never quite landing, never quite safe.

This is why understanding RSD is so important. Not just for those who live with it, but for those around them. Because RSD does not exist in a vacuum. It touches everything; friendships, families, classrooms, workplaces. It can bewilder partners, frustrate colleagues, and confuse clinicians. Without a name, it can look like irrationality. Overreaction. Moodiness. Drama. But with a name, it becomes something else. Understandable. Treatable. Nameable. And that, in itself, is powerful.

The Invisible Blueprint

There is a kind of blueprint that many people with RSD seem to carry; often without knowing it. It's an emotional script that plays out again and again.

1. A social cue is misread or hits a sensitive spot.
2. The person experiences a rapid, disproportionate emotional response.
3. Shame or panic sets in.

4. The person either lashes out, retreats, or dissociates.
5. Later, they replay the moment obsessively, doubting their reaction or questioning their sanity.

This script plays out not just in dramatic episodes, but in quiet ways too. It affects how people interpret text messages, job interviews, social plans, facial expressions. It changes the way they speak, apologise, joke, and love. It is exhausting. And for many, it's been there since childhood.

One of the hardest parts of RSD is the sense that something is wrong; but not being able to explain what. Especially for those who were never diagnosed with ADHD or autism, or who grew up in environments where emotional needs were dismissed, the experience of RSD often hides under other labels: difficult, oversensitive, attention-seeking. By adulthood, many have learned to camouflage their reactions, but that doesn't mean the pain is gone. It just means they've stopped talking about it.

Is It Always Rejection?

This is a question worth pausing on. Not every person with RSD is aware of reacting to "rejection" in the classic sense. Sometimes, what triggers the spiral isn't rejection itself but the fear of it. A glance, a silence, a shift in tone. The nervous system flares up before the mind has time to catch up. The body reacts. The heart races. The inner critic roars.

And it's not just social rejection. Perfectionism often walks hand-in-hand with RSD. Some people fear letting others down so much that they develop a near-obsessive drive to avoid failure. A slightly offhand comment can feel like condemnation. A lukewarm review feels like public humiliation. They seek reassurance not out of vanity, but from deep-seated fear. Not: "Do you like me?" but: "Am I safe?"

So, What Is RSD?

RSD is best understood as a hypersensitivity to perceived social threat. That includes rejection, criticism, disapproval, exclusion, and even ambiguity. It's not always irrational, but it is exaggerated. The emotional reactions are out of proportion not because the person is overreacting, but because their system is wired to respond in this way.

Think of RSD as an overactive alarm system. It goes off at the slightest sign of danger. And when it does, the whole house shuts down. Lights flicker, locks engage, doors slam. It takes time to reset. And during that time, it can be hard to think clearly, speak calmly, or even remember that the threat may not have been real.

But here's the vital piece: once we name this alarm system, we can begin to work with it. We can learn to notice when it's been triggered. We can start to unhook from the automatic spiral. We can gently introduce doubt to the inner critic. And for those who support someone with RSD, understanding the mechanism behind the reaction can shift everything—from defensiveness to compassion, from confusion to clarity.

RSD is not who someone is. It is something they experience. And with awareness, support, and practice, it can become less defining, less dominating, less destructive.

Naming It Is Not Enough (But It's a Start)

One of the first things many people say when they learn the term "Rejection Sensitive Dysphoria" is: That's me. That's what I've been feeling all along. There's relief in finally naming something that has shaped your interactions, your choices, and your inner life for years; maybe decades. But naming it is not the same as healing it.

Recognition offers a doorway, not a destination. It allows a person to go back and look again at moments they once labelled overreactions, drama, shame, or regret. It lets them reinterpret those spirals through a new lens; one that acknowledges pain rather than pathologising it.

But awareness alone doesn't make the sting go away. For many, it raises new questions. What do I do now? How do I explain this to others without sounding fragile? What if people use it against me? How do I tell the difference between real rejection and my fear of it? These are questions this book will return to often. But here, in this opening chapter, the most important thing is this:

You are not broken. You are not weak. And you are certainly not alone.

Why It's So Hard to Spot

If RSD is so intense, why does it often go unnoticed by others? There are a few reasons.

First, many people with RSD are highly functional. They hold jobs, maintain relationships, and perform well; at least outwardly. They've developed strong compensatory strategies. They over-prepare, anticipate reactions, smooth conflict, become deeply attuned to others' moods. Their efforts often pass for perfectionism or people-pleasing. Rarely does someone suspect the deeper pain that drives it.

Second, RSD tends to hide behind other labels. Anxiety. Burnout. Mood swings. Anger issues. Low confidence. Depression. Self-sabotage. These may all be present, but they are often symptoms of an unrecognised pattern rather than stand-alone problems. Even in therapy, unless the clinician is familiar with neurodivergent profiles or emotional regulation difficulties, RSD may not come up by name.

Finally, people with RSD may not talk about it; not because they don't feel it, but because they assume everyone feels this way. Or worse, they think they're the only ones. Either belief isolates them further.

This silence creates a feedback loop. The more a person hides their inner experience, the more "out of nowhere" their emotional reactions seem to others. Which makes them harder to explain. Which increases the shame. And so on.

But Isn't Everyone Afraid of Rejection?

Yes. Of course. Rejection hurts. It's one of the oldest human fears, tied to our survival instincts and our need to belong. No one likes being dismissed, excluded, or criticised. That part is universal.

What makes RSD different is the intensity and immediacy of the emotional response, paired with an internal belief that rejection is inevitable, personal, and unbearable. It's not just, "That hurt." It's, "I'll never be enough." Or, "They hate me now." Or, "I should disappear."

Where most people might feel a sting and then move on, someone with RSD may spiral for hours or days. They may cut off contact, end relationships, quit jobs, or implode emotionally, all from what others would consider minor triggers. And crucially, they often feel ashamed of this reaction, even as they're experiencing it. That self-awareness doesn't lessen the pain. Sometimes it deepens it.

Can You Have RSD Without Real Rejection?

Absolutely. In fact, many of the most painful episodes of RSD are based not on what happened but on what was imagined or anticipated. The brain reacts to possibility as if it were certainty.

This means that even ambiguous cues (eg: a delay in response, a neutral facial expression, a shift in someone's tone) can trigger the same crushing response as outright criticism. The mind fills in the blanks. And once the spiral begins, it's hard to stop.

For this reason, RSD often becomes self-reinforcing. The more someone is afraid of rejection, the more they monitor for signs. The more they monitor, the more they misread. The more they misread, the more they pull away or push others away. And in the end, the feared rejection becomes real.

That doesn't mean it was inevitable. It means the person's nervous system was working overtime to protect them. But in doing so, it created exactly the outcome they feared most: isolation.

Where This Book Is Headed

This chapter has laid the groundwork. We've defined RSD. We've looked at how it plays out, what it feels like, and why it's often missed. But there's much more ahead.

We'll explore the overlap between RSD and neurodivergence; particularly ADHD and autism. We'll examine the impact on relationships, school, work, and self-image. We'll look at how RSD shows up in children and teenagers, and how it changes (or doesn't) in adulthood. Most importantly, we'll explore strategies that help: not to "fix" the person, but to reduce suffering, build awareness, and support healthier ways of living and relating.

This book is not a promise to eliminate RSD. That would be unrealistic and, frankly, unhelpful. But it is a guide toward understanding it. And in understanding it, people can make different choices. They can find ways to pause the spiral, question the panic, build trust, and feel less alone.

Because while rejection will always sting, it doesn't have to destroy.

Chap 2: RSD, Autism and ADHD

When Conditions Collide: Untangling the Knots

Rejection Sensitive Dysphoria, ADHD, and autism are often spoken about together. Sometimes this is helpful. Other times it causes confusion, especially when language gets muddled or assumptions are made. To start clearly: RSD is not officially classified as a disorder. It is not listed in the DSM or ICD. It is a term used to describe a pattern of extreme emotional responses to perceived rejection, criticism, or exclusion.

ADHD and autism, by contrast, are recognised neurodevelopmental conditions. Both affect the way people process information, interact socially, regulate emotion, and respond to their environments. But they do so in distinct ways. And yet, many people with ADHD or autism describe emotional experiences that match the profile of RSD with eerie precision. This overlap is not imagined. It is real. But it is not universal. Understanding the difference matters.

Let's start by drawing lines, not walls. Lines help us see contrast and connection. Walls obscure both.

RSD and ADHD: Emotional Storms in a Skewed System

Among people with ADHD, RSD is frequently cited as one of the most painful and disruptive features of their day-to-day lives. It is not formally part of the diagnostic criteria, but many clinicians and researchers now recognise it as an important part of the emotional regulation challenges that define ADHD.

To understand the connection, we need to talk about brain function. ADHD is often reduced to problems with attention, but that is only one part of a much broader picture. At its core, ADHD involves difficulty with regulation. That includes time, attention, motivation, and especially emotion. People with ADHD often experience emotional reactions that are fast, intense, and hard to control. This is not a failure of willpower or maturity. It is a neurological difference in how the brain handles incoming stimuli.

When someone with ADHD perceives a social threat - a raised eyebrow, a delayed reply, a passing comment - they often feel it more strongly and more immediately than others might. Their nervous system is already primed for urgency. Their thoughts may spiral quickly. Their emotions follow suit. The result is what we call rejection sensitivity. But for some, the reaction is so rapid and so intense that it becomes dysphoria. Not just discomfort. Distress. Shame. Rage. Collapse.

This is RSD.

It is not simply about being hurt by rejection. It is about being undone by it. For someone with ADHD, the emotional aftermath of a perceived slight can last hours or days, disrupting concentration, relationships, and self-worth. In many cases, the perceived rejection was never intended or even real. But the pain is. The response is. And the consequences are lived.

Autism and Rejection: A Different Kind of Sensitivity

Autistic individuals often experience the social world differently. They may find it difficult to interpret subtle cues, shift conversational tone quickly, or navigate the unspoken norms of peer interaction. These challenges are not about lack of interest or empathy, but about cognitive processing differences that affect how social information is perceived, prioritised, and integrated.

The result is that many autistic people report chronic experiences of social rejection. Sometimes this is overt; being excluded, bullied, mocked. Other times it is more subtle. Friends drift away. Colleagues stop including them in group chats. Dates don't call back. The cumulative effect of these experiences is real and often deeply painful.

Where ADHD-related RSD is often fast and explosive, rejection sensitivity in autism can be more internalised. It may look like withdrawal, shutdown, or mask-wearing. Many autistic people describe "toning themselves down" or suppressing natural behaviours in order to fit in. This is known as masking, and it is emotionally exhausting. When masking fails, or when rejection happens anyway, the pain can be overwhelming.

It is easy to assume that autistic people don't feel rejection as strongly simply because they may not always express distress in ways others recognise. This is a mistake. Emotional expression is not the same as emotional depth. In fact, some autistic people report feeling rejection so acutely that they avoid social interaction altogether; not because they don't care, but because they care too much and fear the pain of misunderstanding.

So, is that RSD? In many cases, it fits the emotional profile: intense, disproportionate distress in response to perceived rejection or criticism. But the mechanisms and contexts are often different. For example, an autistic person may not interpret a social slight in the same way someone with ADHD might. They may miss the cue entirely, or they may misattribute its meaning. But once the realisation lands, or once exclusion becomes undeniable, the emotional fallout can be every bit as intense.

The Role of Executive Function and Interpretation

Another factor to consider is executive function: the cognitive system that helps us plan, prioritise, regulate emotion, and reflect. Both ADHD and autism involve executive function differences. But those differences play out in distinct ways.

In ADHD, executive function struggles often appear as impulsivity, difficulty with sustained attention, and emotional reactivity. In autism, they may present as rigidity, difficulty with change, or challenges in processing complex emotional information.

What does this mean for rejection sensitivity?

In ADHD, a perceived rejection may bypass thoughtful interpretation altogether. The feeling lands first. The thought follows, if it arrives at all. This leads to quick, intense responses: lashing out, shutting down, walking away. In autism, the recognition of rejection may come later, sometimes after long analysis. But when it hits, the emotional weight is just as heavy—sometimes heavier because it feels so inescapable, so final, so inexplicable.

When Labels Collide: Who Gets Recognised?

One of the most complicated aspects of discussing RSD in relation to ADHD and autism is how diagnosis influences access to understanding, treatment, and even self-compassion.

Many people with RSD symptoms never receive an ADHD or autism diagnosis. They may be high-functioning, masked, or misdiagnosed. Girls and women, in particular, are often overlooked, especially if they internalise their distress rather than externalise it. This invisibility delays recognition of RSD. When no one sees the underlying neurodivergence, the person is often labelled "too emotional," "hypersensitive," or "unstable" which only compounds the shame and isolation.

On the other hand, some individuals are diagnosed with ADHD or autism but never learn about RSD as a possible explanation for their social-emotional struggles. Their meltdowns get attributed to stress. Their withdrawal is blamed on depression. The sharpness of their reactions is framed as a character issue. Without language for the emotional fallout of rejection, many are left without tools to respond or recover.

This is why the question "Can you have RSD without ADHD or autism?" matters so much. Not to gatekeep. Not to exclude. But to clarify. Understanding where RSD shows up, and why, is the first step to helping people navigate it.

Can You Have RSD Without ADHD or Autism?

The short answer is yes. But the explanation deserves care. While RSD is strongly associated with ADHD and, to a lesser extent, autism, it is not exclusive to those conditions. People without any formal diagnosis of neurodivergence can and do experience patterns that mirror RSD. The reasons are varied, and often complex.

For some, chronic rejection in early relationships creates a heightened sensitivity to future exclusion. This can happen in families where love is conditional, in schools where bullying is persistent, or in cultures where emotional expression is punished. Over time, the person learns to scan for threat, anticipate hurt, and catastrophise small social cues. Their brain becomes wired to expect rejection, and their body responds accordingly.

This can look a lot like RSD. The intensity is there. The shutdown, the shame, the emotional flood - it all fits. But the root is different. It is not neurological so much as relational. This doesn't make the pain any less real. Nor does it mean it is "just trauma." The overlap between RSD and complex trauma is real, and it often blurs.

There's also a growing conversation around attachment style and its connection to rejection sensitivity. People with anxious attachment, for example, may experience deep distress at perceived abandonment or criticism. While this isn't RSD in the neurological sense, it can feel very similar. And it may respond better to different interventions, ones focused on relationship patterns and self-regulation, rather than executive function or sensory input.

So the answer is yes. You can have RSD-like reactions without ADHD or autism. But to know how to respond, to support someone or to support yourself, it helps to understand what is feeding the sensitivity. Where there's overlap, it should be named. Where there's difference, it should be respected. No single explanation fits everyone.

The Risk of Over-pathologising

With growing awareness of RSD comes the risk of overusing the label. Not everyone who dislikes rejection is experiencing RSD. Not everyone who has a bad reaction to criticism is neurodivergent. And not every emotionally intense person is "dysphoric."

This matters because when terms like RSD become too loosely applied, they lose meaning. People stop being taken seriously. Real suffering gets dismissed as trend. And those who most need help get drowned in noise.

At the same time, we must avoid the opposite trap: assuming RSD is rare or illegitimate because it lacks formal status in diagnostic manuals. Lived experience matters. So does clinical insight. Many seasoned practitioners now recognise RSD as a real and specific pattern, one that requires nuance, care, and attention.

For clinicians, this means looking past labels and listening closely to the story being told. For family and friends, it means holding space for emotional intensity without assuming manipulation or overreaction. For those who live with it, it means understanding the landscape of your own emotional system; its roots, its triggers, and its rhythms.

Shared Threads, Distinct Patterns

RSD, ADHD, and autism share common terrain, but they are not the same road. They overlap most clearly in emotional reactivity and sensitivity to perceived social threat. But the drivers behind those reactions differ.

ADHD often brings impulsivity and emotional dysregulation to the forefront. The reaction is quick. The system floods fast. The shame sets in before thought can intervene. This pattern creates a cycle of volatility and self-recrimination that wears down relationships and self-esteem.

Autism, by contrast, often involves cumulative pain. The rejection isn't always tied to single moments. It comes from years of misunderstanding. Years of watching others connect with ease while you struggle to decode the rules. Years of being told you're too blunt, too quiet, too intense, too odd. The rejection lands in quieter ways, but it lands deeply. The resulting sensitivity may not look explosive.

But it can lead to social paralysis, chronic masking, and emotional exhaustion.

In both cases, the nervous system becomes hyper-attuned to social threat. But the outward behaviour may vary. One person may lash out, another may shut down. One might become people-pleasing to a fault. Another may retreat into solitude, convinced connection is too painful to attempt.

RSD adds a layer to this picture. It isn't a formal condition. But it acts like a lens; a way of explaining why the emotional landscape is so volatile in the context of rejection, disapproval, or even imagined social slights.

Why It Matters for Treatment and Support

Understanding these distinctions isn't just academic. It changes how we help people.

If RSD is showing up in the context of ADHD, tools that support executive function, impulse control, and emotional self-awareness are often helpful. These might include ADHD coaching, medication that targets emotional dysregulation, or techniques rooted in behavioural therapy that support pause and reflection.

If RSD is present alongside autism, support may need to focus more on sensory regulation, social fatigue, and the relief of authentic expression without masking. Autistic people often benefit from clear social feedback, flexible expectations, and relationships that do not punish difference.

And if RSD shows up without either ADHD or autism, support may need to focus more on healing attachment wounds, reframing internal narratives, or processing trauma. The interventions change, but the underlying compassion remains the same.

A one-size-fits-all approach will fail. What's needed is clarity. Clarity allows for targeted, personalised support. It prevents shame. It creates options. And for many, it is the beginning of real change.

The Cost of Misunderstanding

When RSD is missed, relationships suffer. A child labelled difficult may instead be overwhelmed by emotional noise. A student who seems oppositional may be desperately trying to protect themselves from public humiliation. A partner who overreacts to a neutral comment may be reliving hundreds of moments where criticism meant abandonment.

If we fail to recognise the mechanism behind these reactions, we are left only with the behaviour. And behaviour out of context is easy to judge. But behaviour in context is something else entirely. It becomes information. It becomes understandable. And, crucially, it becomes workable.

Final Thoughts: From Confusion to Clarity

The question is not just who has RSD. The question is what lies beneath it. Is it driven by neurodivergent wiring? By long-standing trauma? By relational patterns built in childhood? By sensory overload? Likely, it's a combination of factors. That's why this chapter does not aim to offer neat boxes or easy answers.

It aims to offer a map.

That map includes overlap between ADHD and autism, between rejection and regulation, between neurological difference and emotional survival. But it also includes divergence. Not every autistic person is emotionally reactive. Not every person with ADHD has RSD. Not every adult who struggles with shame and criticism is neurodivergent.

The goal is not to label but to illuminate. If someone you love reacts more sharply to rejection than you expect, ask why. If you find yourself avoiding opportunities because you can't bear the risk of failure, ask where that belief was born. If someone shuts down when challenged, don't assume it's defiance. It might be pain.

RSD is not the whole story. But it's a vital part of many stories. And when we understand its connection to ADHD and autism, not as a rule, but as a recurring pattern, we begin to see people more fully. We begin to offer support, not pressure. Clarity, not confusion. Repair, not rejection.

And that is where real connection begins.

Chap 3: What Triggers RSD Episodes?

The Lightning Rod Effect: How RSD Reacts to Everyday Life

For many people with Rejection Sensitive Dysphoria, the world feels like an emotional minefield. Situations that others might breeze through - like receiving delayed feedback from a boss or sensing a friend's impatience - can jolt the nervous system like an electric shock. The trigger doesn't have to be dramatic. It can be as subtle as a glance, a shift in tone, a perceived pause in a conversation, or the absence of a smile. These moments become highly charged for someone with RSD, activating an internal alarm system that's often more reactive than reflective.

What makes a trigger a trigger isn't always the event itself. It's the interpretation; the lens through which a person experiences social signals. That lens is shaped by years of emotional wiring, sensitivity to approval, fear of disconnection, and a deeply entrenched belief that they are on the edge of being judged or rejected at any moment. And crucially, this reaction is not a conscious choice. It's automatic, overwhelming, and often occurs before the person even realizes what's happening.

People with RSD are not simply "too sensitive." They are living with a nervous system calibrated to detect threat in the form of disapproval, detachment, or perceived failure. The resulting emotions (shame, panic, grief, self-loathing etc) can arise instantly, even in moments that seem entirely mundane to others.

Common Triggers That Spark Disproportionate Pain

Let's explore some of the most frequent triggers that tend to set off RSD responses:

- Delayed responses or silence: Waiting on a reply to a message or email can be agonizing. The delay feels like avoidance or rejection. A blank screen becomes a mirror for shame and uncertainty. The mind fills in the blanks with worst-case scenarios.

- Mild criticism: Even gentle or constructive feedback can cut deeply. A teacher's suggestion, a supervisor's correction, or a loved one's teasing remark may feel like devastating proof of failure or inadequacy.
- Social exclusion or perceived neglect: Being left out of a conversation, overlooked in a group, or not invited to something others are attending can stir an overwhelming sense of being unwanted or unloved—even when there was no malicious intent behind it.
- Shifts in tone or expression: A friend sounding more formal than usual, or a partner seeming preoccupied, can be misread as anger, disapproval, or abandonment.
- Romantic uncertainty: Mixed messages, postponed dates, or lukewarm responses can trigger intense self-doubt and emotional distress. The emotional stakes feel impossibly high, especially in the early stages of connection.
- Lack of affirmation: For some, the absence of reassurance or praise feels like withdrawal of affection. Silence is interpreted not as neutral, but as negative.

Each of these examples represents a kind of emotional misfire. The nervous system receives a cue and magnifies it into something much larger, something dangerous. And once that internal switch is flipped, it becomes difficult to regulate the response.

Triggers Are Personal, Not Universal

It's important to understand that RSD triggers are highly individual. What shatters one person might barely register for another. One person might be undone by a partner canceling dinner plans. Another might spiral after a coworker fails to greet them in the hallway.

The trigger doesn't need to be logical. It needs only to feel like rejection. And that feeling often bypasses reason entirely.

This is part of what makes RSD so invisible to others. Friends or partners may be baffled by what seems like an overreaction. They may even become defensive or irritated. "I didn't mean it that way." "You're taking it too personally." "You're reading into things." But the pain is real. The body responds with the same flood of cortisol and adrenaline it would produce in a moment of actual threat. A simple oversight can feel like exile.

This disconnect between lived experience and outside perception can compound the shame for someone with RSD. Not only do they feel hurt, but they often feel ridiculous for being hurt. They may learn to mask it, to keep their reactions private, or to preemptively withdraw in order to avoid potential rejection. That kind of emotional preloading (constantly scanning for danger) is exhausting, and it narrows their world.

Emotional Memory Makes Triggers More Potent

Another reason RSD triggers hit so hard is the role of emotional memory. The brain stores not just the facts of a previous rejection but the feeling of it. And when something in the present moment reminds the nervous system, consciously or not, of a past injury, the emotional residue of that old wound is reactivated.

This isn't always clear to the person experiencing it. They might not consciously remember the time their teacher humiliated them in front of the class, or when they were left out of a childhood birthday party. But their body remembers. Their threat detection system remembers. So when a colleague makes a cutting remark in a meeting or a group chat goes silent, the reaction may seem wildly disproportionate, unless you understand what's being carried inside.

RSD episodes are often cumulative in this way. A present-day trigger is like a spark landing on a dry forest floor. The ignition is instantaneous. And the fire that follows isn't just about this moment. It's about every moment that ever felt like it.

The Trigger Chain: One Moment Can Set Off Many

Sometimes, it's not a single incident that causes the emotional storm. It's a sequence. The mind starts with a small observation: "She didn't reply." which quickly cascades into meaning-making: "She's annoyed with me." "I must have said something wrong." "She's going to stop speaking to me." Before long, the person is caught in a narrative loop of self-blame, doom, and inner collapse.

Once that emotional chain reaction begins, it becomes difficult to intervene. The brain is now in a threat state, the body is tense, the stomach knots, the mind narrows. The internal monologue turns vicious: "You're too much." "You always mess things up." "No one wants you around."

This spiral can unfold in a matter of seconds. And once it takes hold, the trigger may become irrelevant. The focus shifts inward. The person may begin replaying other moments of failure, scanning their history for evidence of being unlovable or disappointing. One small incident now feels like confirmation of everything they feared was true about themselves.

Silence Is Often the Loudest Trigger

For many people with RSD, non-response can be more distressing than overt criticism. A lack of reply to a message. A pause in conversation. A change in tone. These subtle absences become loaded with meaning. Silence is rarely neutral to someone with RSD. It quickly becomes a canvas onto which the mind paints rejection.

The waiting itself is agony. While others might interpret a delayed reply as forgetfulness or busyness, someone with RSD may interpret it as personal withdrawal. They begin to fill in the blanks with self-directed narratives: "They're ignoring me." "They don't want to deal with me." "They've had enough."

These spirals don't come from insecurity alone. They arise because the nervous system has been conditioned to view uncertainty as dangerous. In the absence of reassurance, the brain fills the gap with worst-case scenarios. That gap becomes the trigger.

It's important to note that silence doesn't need to come from someone close. It might be a professional contact who doesn't answer a follow-up. A teacher who takes too long to return a marked assignment. A group that doesn't reply in a chat. The mind seizes on the vacuum and fills it with rejection.

Even Praise Can Be a Trigger

This may seem paradoxical, but positive attention can also activate RSD. Why? Because praise often raises the stakes. It creates pressure to maintain that standard, to never disappoint, to never fall from grace. For someone with RSD, a compliment can become a setup for future rejection.

Let's say a person is told they did an excellent job on a presentation. Instead of feeling proud, they may feel dread. What if I can't do that well next time? What if I only succeeded by accident? What if they're expecting more than I can deliver?

These thoughts aren't mere impostor syndrome. They're the front edge of rejection sensitivity. The person isn't basking in the glow of approval—they're bracing for its withdrawal. Even warmth can become a threat if it carries an implicit demand.

This is especially common in high-achieving individuals with RSD. They may constantly strive to earn praise, but be unable to enjoy it. Every success feels like a momentary stay of execution. Praise becomes a trap: enjoy it, and you risk relaxing. Relax, and you might slip up. Slip up, and the rejection you've feared will come crashing down.

Triggers in Close Relationships

RSD is often most pronounced in close emotional relationships, where vulnerability runs deepest. A mildly critical comment from a partner can feel like a gut punch. An attempt at honest feedback can spiral into devastation. Even a neutral facial expression can be misread as disappointment.

This hypersensitivity doesn't come from a lack of love or care. In fact, it often comes from the intensity of that love. When someone matters deeply, their opinions carry enormous weight. For people with RSD, any sign of disapproval from someone close is felt on a cellular level. It becomes hard to distinguish between momentary frustration and outright abandonment.

This puts pressure on both parties. The person with RSD may feel ashamed of their reactions and try to suppress them. Their partner, friend, or parent may walk on eggshells, worried about triggering a spiral. Without understanding what's really happening, both sides may feel confused and exhausted.

Open dialogue can help. So can external validation from a therapist or support group. But the first step is recognising that these reactions are not flaws in character—they are expressions of nervous system sensitivity, born of past pain and wired through experience.

Feedback Fatigue: When "Helpful" Hurts

Constructive feedback is part of nearly every personal, academic, and professional relationship. But for someone with RSD, even kindly worded or well-intentioned suggestions can feel wounding. A passing remark like "Next time, try using a stronger opening" may register not as guidance, but as condemnation.

This is not about being overly sensitive in a casual way. It's about the nervous system perceiving correction as rejection. Even the idea that something could have been done better can spark a full cascade of emotional pain. Not because the person lacks resilience, but because their system is primed to interpret even small signals as threats to belonging or approval.

Over time, this creates what we might call feedback fatigue; a growing inability to tolerate evaluations of any kind. Teachers and supervisors often misinterpret this as defensiveness or an unwillingness to learn. In reality, the person with RSD may desperately want to improve. But the cost of hearing they've fallen short is so great that they begin to avoid feedback altogether.

They may stop asking for input. They may procrastinate on tasks that will be reviewed. They may even self-sabotage or "beat others to the punch" by openly criticising their own work before anyone else can. This is an attempt at control: if I name the flaw first, maybe it won't hurt as much.

The Fear of Being an Inconvenience

One of the most quietly devastating RSD triggers is the sense of being a burden. Many people with RSD live with a constant background fear: What if I'm annoying them? What if I'm asking too much? What if I'm too emotional, too needy, too intense?

These thoughts often emerge in small, everyday moments. Sending a second text when someone hasn't replied. Needing help with a task. Asking for reassurance after a difficult day. Any of these might be entirely normal in most relationships, but for someone with RSD, they feel fraught with risk. The person may agonise before reaching out. Then, if the response isn't immediate or warm, they may spiral into self-blame and shame.

This creates a deep internal conflict. The person longs for connection but fears that their needs will push people away. So they suppress their feelings, downplay their struggles, and try to take up as little space as possible. Ironically, this can make relationships more strained -not less - as their true emotions leak out in other ways: resentment, withdrawal, or sudden outbursts.

Over time, this pattern can lead to emotional burnout. The effort to seem "low-maintenance" becomes unsustainable, especially during periods of stress or crisis. And when the person finally does break down, they often feel humiliated or convinced they've ruined the relationship.

Sensory and Environmental Triggers

While most RSD triggers are emotional or social, some are contextual or sensory. A chaotic workplace. A noisy classroom. A disorganised group project. Environments like these don't cause RSD, but they can raise the emotional temperature enough to make a rejection episode more likely.

Many people with RSD also experience traits associated with ADHD, autism, or sensory processing differences. In these cases, external overstimulation - too much light, noise, or unpredictability - can make emotional regulation even harder. The person may already be using significant energy just to stay focused or calm. Add a social misunderstanding or a perceived slight on top of that, and the system can tip into overwhelm.

This is often misunderstood. Someone may appear "overreactive" to a simple change in schedule or a teacher's tone of voice. But what others don't see is the invisible effort it took just to stay regulated up to that point. The trigger may seem small, but it's falling on an already-taxed nervous system. The explosion is often the result of accumulation, not just the final spark.

When Support Itself Feels Threatening

In many relationships, offering support is a sign of care. But for someone with RSD, receiving help can be its own kind of trigger. Being comforted, reassured, or "talked down" after a distressing event might make them feel weak or exposed. There's a sense that being comforted confirms the worst fear: I'm not okay. I can't handle life. I'm too much.

This paradox, needing connection but fearing what it says about you, can make it very difficult to let others in. The person might push support away even when they desperately need it. Or they might feel flooded with shame immediately after being vulnerable, replaying the interaction in their mind and judging themselves for "oversharing."

The same applies in therapeutic settings. Many people with RSD are highly self-aware. They might nod along with their therapist, understand the tools, and still walk out feeling humiliated for having cried, gotten angry, or even just shown emotion. It's not that the therapy didn't help. It's that their inner critic interprets their openness as a kind of social failure.

This dynamic often requires naming explicitly: "Accepting support does not make you weak." For someone with RSD, that message may need to be repeated often and reinforced with action—calm, consistent, non-judgmental presence from others who don't flinch when the mask slips.

The Final Layer: Self as Trigger

Perhaps the most painful truth is that sometimes, the biggest RSD trigger is the self. Many people with RSD are not only reacting to external signals of rejection but also carrying deep internalised beliefs about being unworthy, broken, or defective.

These beliefs can be old, rooted in years of social confusion, school struggles, relationship friction, or feeling "different" without understanding why. Over time, the person internalises these patterns. They begin to expect rejection. To assume that if something goes wrong, it's their fault. That if someone pulls away, it's because of who they are at the core.

This creates a feedback loop. Even when nothing overt has happened, the mere possibility of rejection can stir up old wounds. A delay in a reply. A neutral facial expression. A vague comment. These can all be interpreted through the lens of past pain. And because the pain is real and intense, the brain treats the situation as confirmation, reinforcing the narrative: "See? I knew they didn't really like me."

Breaking this loop requires more than logic. It demands emotional safety, patient self-inquiry, and often a slow rebuilding of identity. The person with RSD must learn not just to manage their reactions, but to question the story they tell themselves about who they are.

That is a long road. But it begins with awareness. Understanding what triggers RSD episodes is not about avoidance or blame. It's about clarity. And from clarity comes power—the power to pause, to reframe, and to rewrite the script that has governed so many interactions for so long.

Chap 4: The Biology of Emotional Pain

The Human Nervous System Wasn't Built for This

Let's begin with something simple but important: the human brain is old. Not in years, but in architecture. It evolved over hundreds of thousands of years to keep us alive in environments that were utterly unlike the one we live in today. Back then, rejection could literally be fatal. If you were cast out from your tribe or community, you weren't just facing loneliness, you were facing predators, exposure, starvation. Our nervous system developed to treat social exclusion as an emergency.

This evolutionary backdrop still influences how our bodies function now. When someone with Rejection Sensitive Dysphoria (RSD) perceives rejection (even if it's imagined, subtle, or unintentional) their body doesn't treat it as a small interpersonal hiccup. It interprets it as a full-blown threat. This is not melodrama or weakness. It's not overreaction or fragility. It's the legacy of a brain doing exactly what it was wired to do: protect.

For people with RSD, this response is intensified. The amygdala, the part of the brain that signals danger, flares up like a smoke alarm that's been set too close to the toaster. The body goes into a stress response that is far out of proportion to the external stimulus but completely in proportion to the inner wiring that the person didn't choose and cannot easily override.

Pain That Feels Physical (Because It Is)

One of the most misunderstood things about RSD is just how physical it feels. People often describe it as an emotional "sting" or a sharp, aching pain. But this isn't a metaphor. Neuroscience confirms that social pain and physical pain share many of the same neural pathways.

The anterior cingulate cortex, for example, is active in both physical injury and emotional distress. When someone with RSD experiences rejection, this part of the brain lights up in a way that resembles being punched in the chest. The pain is not imagined. It's not symbolic. It is real, lived, and embodied.

And yet, it is invisible. That's part of the cruelty. People who break a leg are met with sympathy. People who wince at a perceived slight are often met with scorn or confusion. The biology of emotional pain makes no such distinctions. It just hurts. And for someone with RSD, it hurts deeply and immediately; often before they've had a chance to rationalise or reality-check what's happening.

The Speed of the Reaction

The emotional response to perceived rejection in someone with RSD is not just intense, it's fast. In a fraction of a second, their body floods with cortisol and adrenaline. Their heart rate spikes. Breathing becomes shallow. Muscles tighten. This is a biological cascade, not a voluntary reaction.

Many describe the sensation as being hijacked by their own nervous system. One moment they are in a normal interaction. The next, they are spiralling, unable to concentrate, speak, or stay present. Their brain has triggered a fight, flight, or freeze response over something that others might not even notice.

This reactivity doesn't reflect immaturity or lack of coping skills. It reflects a nervous system that's wired to protect against threats that no longer exist in the same form—but still register with the same force.

Why Logic Doesn't Work in the Moment

One of the most frustrating things about emotional pain, especially for those around the person experiencing it, is that logic often fails to help in the moment. You can explain, rationalise, reassure, but it's like trying to calm a fire with paperwork. The body is already in a state of alarm. The reasoning part of the brain, the prefrontal cortex, is not driving the bus anymore.

In fact, people with RSD often know that their reaction is out of proportion. They know the email wasn't meant as a slight. They know the teacher didn't mean to embarrass them. They know the tone in their friend's voice probably had nothing to do with them. But they feel the rejection anyway, and that feeling hits before any thought can catch up.

This is biology. The brain prioritises survival over accuracy. That's true for all of us, but for those with RSD, the survival systems are hair-triggered. The same way some people have sensitive skin or overreactive allergies, people with RSD have nervous systems that perceive social threat too easily and too powerfully.

The Invisible Toll on Energy and Function

Because the nervous system is working overtime, people with RSD often live with a constant background hum of tension. Their muscles may be tight without them realising it. Sleep may be restless. Their mind may race through imaginary conversations or perceived slights, unable to turn down the volume on those intrusive thoughts.

This takes an enormous toll on energy. Emotional labour is exhausting at the best of times, but when the nervous system is in a repeated state of red alert, fatigue becomes inevitable. People with RSD may appear avoidant, lazy, or moody from the outside. But internally, they may be using tremendous energy just to regulate themselves enough to show up.

This internal strain also affects executive function. The brain's ability to plan, prioritise, remember, and focus is severely compromised when emotional systems are activated. That's why RSD often mimics or overlaps with ADHD in terms of attention and motivation—it's not that the person is unwilling or uninterested. It's that their brain is busy putting out fires others can't see.

Overactive Alarm Bells: The Amygdala and RSD

To understand why emotional pain in RSD is so immediate and overwhelming, we need to talk about the amygdala. This almond-shaped structure deep in the brain plays a central role in how we process fear, threat, and strong emotion. In a sense, the amygdala is like a smoke detector for danger. Its job is to fire off an alert when something seems risky or hostile.

For people with RSD, that detector is hypersensitive. It doesn't wait for a full fire to break out. It goes off when there's just a bit of smoke; sometimes even steam from the kettle. The amygdala in RSD-prone individuals is often hyper-reactive, interpreting ambiguous or mildly negative cues as serious threats.

You walk into a room and someone doesn't look up right away? The amygdala might flag it as disapproval. A friend is slow to reply to your text? It registers as abandonment. A teacher corrects your answer in front of others? It triggers shame, even humiliation. This isn't dramatization or mis-interpretation, it's the amygdala doing its job too enthusiastically.

When the amygdala reacts, it bypasses the slower, reasoning parts of the brain. That's why RSD can feel like being ambushed by emotion. It doesn't wait for confirmation or reflection. It just launches a survival response, flooding the body with stress hormones and setting off a physiological chain reaction.

The Brain's Slow Brake: Why Recovery Takes Time

Even after the moment of perceived rejection has passed, the body doesn't instantly reset. The nervous system needs time to wind down. For people with RSD, this recovery period can be painfully slow. Hours - or even days - might pass before their body and mind return to a state of calm.

Why so long? Because cortisol, the stress hormone, remains in the bloodstream well after the event. It disrupts sleep, appetite, digestion, and attention. The body stays braced, waiting for another blow, even when none is coming.

This prolonged state of alertness can lead to emotional burnout. It's like revving a car engine for hours—it's not sustainable. People with RSD may retreat, shut down, or become irritable not because they're avoiding life, but because their system is desperately trying to preserve what little emotional fuel remains.

To others, this might look like overreaction or moodiness. But from the inside, it's more like trying to drive with the brakes on. Everything takes more effort, and small demands feel overwhelming.

Social Pain Leaves a Memory Trace

Another important aspect of the biology of emotional pain is memory. The hippocampus, a region of the brain involved in storing long-term memories, is deeply intertwined with emotional experience. In people with RSD, emotionally painful experiences, especially those involving rejection, are more likely to be encoded strongly and vividly.

This means that perceived slights from the past are often not just remembered but relived. A comment from years ago can still sting when recalled. The brain brings back not just the event but the emotional charge, as if it's happening again in the present moment.

This tendency can make social situations feel dangerous even when they're not. If someone laughed at you once when you gave an opinion in a meeting, your brain may catalogue that memory and then warn you every time you speak up again. The original wound hasn't healed cleanly. It left a scar the brain keeps tracing over.

This isn't stubbornness or unwillingness to "let go." It's the result of a system that is trying to protect you, again, doing what it was designed to do, but doing it too often, and too intensely, for the world we live in.

The Role of the Autonomic Nervous System: Fight, Flight, Freeze... and Fawn

When a person with RSD perceives rejection, the reaction is not just emotional. It's physical. That's because the autonomic nervous system, especially the sympathetic branch, kicks into high gear. This system controls involuntary body functions like heart rate, respiration, blood pressure, and digestion. Its job is to prepare the body for survival when it senses danger.

The classic stress responses (fight, flight, and freeze) are well known. Less well known is the fourth "F": fawn. Many people with RSD experience this. Instead of fighting back, running away, or shutting down, they try to soothe or appease the perceived source of rejection. They might apologise unnecessarily, over-explain, or try too hard to "fix" things, even when they've done nothing wrong.

All four responses are driven by the same internal biology. Heart rate increases. Muscles tense. Breathing becomes shallow. Pupils dilate. Blood moves away from digestion and toward large muscle groups. None of this is conscious. The body is simply acting on ancient cues, interpreting social threat as literal danger.

And here's the kicker: the body doesn't distinguish between emotional and physical threat. The nervous system responds to a hostile email or a friend's silence with the same machinery it would use if you were being chased. It's no wonder people with RSD feel exhausted. Their bodies are doing the equivalent of emergency drills, sometimes dozens of times a day.

Neurotransmitters and Sensitivity: The Chemistry of Overwhelm

There's growing evidence that neurotransmitter activity in the brain may also help explain why RSD feels so intense. Neurotransmitters are chemical messengers that help regulate mood, attention, reward, and pain. Dopamine and norepinephrine, both key players in ADHD, are especially relevant here.

People with ADHD, for instance, often have lower baseline levels of dopamine. This affects not just attention but also emotional regulation. Dopamine helps with motivation, pleasure, and reward prediction. When dopamine is dysregulated, the brain struggles to maintain a sense of emotional balance.

This helps explain why people with RSD can swing so quickly from feeling okay to feeling devastated. A single perceived slight can drain the system of its emotional reserves. It's not because they're fragile. It's because the brain chemistry that normally acts as a buffer is already stretched thin.

Norepinephrine, meanwhile, is involved in the body's stress response. It contributes to arousal, vigilance, and alertness. When rejection is perceived, norepinephrine levels can spike, intensifying the feeling of alarm. This contributes to the sense of being "flooded"; emotionally hijacked, unable to think clearly, or even to speak.

Some researchers also speculate that serotonin, the mood stabilizer, plays a role. Though the exact mechanisms are still under study, what's clear is this: the brain chemistry involved in RSD is not weak. It's overactive. The emotional pain is real, measurable, and driven by biological processes, not character flaws.

Why Logic Doesn't Help in the Moment

It's natural to want to reason your way out of emotional overwhelm. "I know they probably didn't mean it that way." "I'm probably just being sensitive." "I should just let it go." But when the emotional brain is in charge, the logical brain is largely offline.

This isn't a failure of maturity or mindfulness. It's simply how the brain prioritises resources under perceived threat. The prefrontal cortex (the part of the brain responsible for reasoning, planning, and emotional regulation) is slower to activate than the limbic system, where the amygdala resides. By the time you're trying to talk yourself down, the alarm has already sounded and the house is filling with smoke.

That's why people with RSD often say things like, "I knew it wasn't a big deal, but I couldn't stop spiralling." The intellectual part of the brain can understand that the situation doesn't warrant a meltdown. But the nervous system isn't convinced. It's still acting like the threat is real.

This gap between knowing and feeling is one of the most frustrating parts of living with RSD. It's also one of the most misunderstood by others. People might say, "You're overreacting," or

"Just calm down." But that's like telling someone in a burning house to stop breathing in smoke. It's not that simple.

Why It Lingers: The Biology of a Post-Rejection Hangover

Even after the moment has passed; after the text is clarified, the awkward glance explained, or the silence broken, the emotional aftermath can linger. This isn't just rumination. It's biological residue.

After a perceived rejection, the body takes time to return to baseline. Cortisol levels (the body's main stress hormone) remain elevated for hours, sometimes longer. Sleep gets disrupted. Appetite changes. Memory and focus may feel impaired. This is the post-rejection hangover, and it's not imagined.

For many with RSD, the nervous system seems slower to "downregulate." What might be a brief sting for someone else becomes a full-body, full-day ordeal. This is not about choice. It's about how long the brain and body take to feel safe again.

This hangover effect is one reason some people with RSD begin to avoid social interactions altogether. If every minor misstep feels like a gut-punch and takes all day to recover from, it makes sense to limit exposure. But over time, this self-protective strategy can lead to isolation, which in turn amplifies the pain of rejection when it inevitably comes.

Why This Isn't Just "Being Too Sensitive"

One of the most damaging myths around RSD is that it's just about being too sensitive or too thin-skinned. That framing is not only dismissive. It's scientifically inaccurate.

Sensitivity, in the traditional sense, is often framed as a temperament trait. But RSD isn't about personality. It's about physiological reactivity. It's about neural networks that interpret threat with a hair-trigger. It's about a nervous system that was designed for survival, now trying to function in a world where rejection is constant, subtle, and sometimes algorithmically generated.

RSD also differs from standard social anxiety. It's not fear of social situations. It's fear of rejection, real or perceived, often after the fact. It's not a steady hum of worry but a sudden, sharp spike of distress. It doesn't always show up in observable behaviour, either. Many with RSD appear calm and competent on the outside while experiencing internal chaos.

Framing RSD as a flaw, especially in environments like school, work, or relationships, only deepens the cycle. When someone is told they are too sensitive, they learn to mask. They try to suppress their reactions. But suppression is not regulation. It only delays the inevitable explosion or implosion.

Understanding the biology of emotional pain helps reframe the conversation. It moves the narrative from "What's wrong with me?" to "What's happening in me?" That shift opens the door to better strategies, better conversations, and better care.

Chap 5: Daily Life with RSD

Morning to Night: How RSD Shapes a Day

Rejection Sensitive Dysphoria does not arrive with a calendar invitation. It sits in the room as the day begins, shaping what a person notices and what they brace for. Many people wake before their alarm with a pulse that feels half a beat too fast. The mind has already started running background checks on every risk of disapproval that might be waiting outside the bedroom door or on the other side of a phone screen.

Consider a teenager who checks messages before breakfast. A friend sent something late at night, and the thread now shows a small indicator that the message was seen. There is no reply yet. The teen's chest tightens. He imagines he has said something foolish. None of this has happened in reality, but the body treats the possibility as if it were fact. Appetite fades. It is hard to sit at the table and answer ordinary questions about the school day when the nervous system is primed for social danger.

Adults describe a similar start. Work email is a row of unopened envelopes that might contain criticism, or worse, silence. Silence is the most corrosive when you live with RSD. It is quickly translated as rejection, even when the sender is simply in a meeting. That translation is not a moral failing. It is a rapid protective reflex, built to keep a person safe from loss of belonging.

Mornings also carry demands that can feel sharper than they look. Getting children out the door, commuting, answering early messages, checking calendars. Each small task is an opportunity to miss a cue, forget a detail, or be judged for a perceived slip. People with RSD often develop micro rituals to regain control. The mug goes in the same spot. The bag is zipped in a set order. These are not superstitions. They are anchors that stop the day from rolling them out to sea.

By mid-morning a person may already have spent significant mental energy on prediction and prevention. They have drafted and redrafted a message to make sure it sounds right. They have replayed last night's conversation in their head and cut it into pieces to see where it might have gone wrong. If nothing obvious has gone wrong, the mind still checks for what could be hiding. The effort is invisible to others. The weariness is not.

Midday brings its own tests. A meeting where cameras are on. A teacher who glances at the clock. A manager who says, "Can we talk later," with no further detail. A partner who is short in a text because they are also juggling a deadline. Each of these moments is small, but each can feel like a door that might slam. The body prepares for the slam. Shoulders lift. Breathing shortens. The person does their best to look calm and capable while scanning for safety exits.

Evening should be a time to unwind. For many with RSD it is the time when the day plays back at double speed. The brain builds a highlight reel of possible mistakes and missed signals. A minor comment becomes a thread that is pulled at until the whole jumper unravels in the mind. Sleep is delayed. When sleep comes it may be shallow. The morning cycle waits on the other side, ready to begin again.

This picture is not universal, but the themes are common: anticipation, rapid emotional spikes, and a sustained effort to stay inside the circle of acceptance. The aim of this chapter is not to pathologise ordinary worry. It is to name the scale and frequency of the load carried by people with RSD. Naming that load is not the same as surrender to it. With accurate language, patterns become visible, and once they are visible, they can be worked with.

The Small Things That Sting

People often ask why tiny moments cut so deeply. The answer lies in speed and salience. The RSD nervous system tags social threat as high priority. A sigh, a pause, a flat tone, a delay in response. The tag is applied in a fraction of a second, before reflection has time to weigh alternatives. The person then spends minutes or hours trying to undo a first impression that the body treated as fact.

Picture a barista who seems brisk because the queue is long. The customer with RSD leaves with coffee and with a fresh theory that they were rude without knowing it. In the afternoon the scene returns, sharper than before. By evening the theory has grown roots. A friend might say, "It was nothing." That sentence stops the conversation rather than helping it. To the person with RSD it was not nothing. It was a small cut in a place already thin from many cuts.

Digital life multiplies these small cuts. Icons change colour. Read receipts arrive without replies. An email lands with no greeting. A colleague reacts to a message in a group chat but not to yours. Each cue is ambiguous, which means each cue is open to the harshest possible interpretation. The harsh interpretation arrives first, and it comes with an ache behind the ribs that is hard to explain to people who do not feel it.

The fear is not simply of being disliked. It is the fear of exclusion. Human beings survive in groups. The brain treats exclusion as a threat to survival, and the pain map reflects that. People with RSD are often extremely loyal and deeply caring. Their sensitivity comes from a wish to protect connection, not to demand special treatment. Yet the world can read their intensity as neediness, and that misreading can add another layer of hurt.

These small stings accumulate. By night a person can feel used up by a day that looked ordinary from the outside. They may cancel an evening plan, not because they do not want company, but because they have no spare capacity left for the risk that company brings. Loved ones sometimes feel confused by the cancellations. No one sees the ledger where a hundred tiny charges have already been entered since breakfast.

Coping in Social Spaces

Social life is the place where RSD is most visible to the person who lives with it and least visible to everyone else. The person stands in a group and tracks facial expressions as if scanning a control panel. A raised eyebrow is logged. A yawn is logged. A glance away at the exact moment you speak is logged. The log fills with data points that all point to one conclusion: you are falling out of favour. That conclusion may have no basis in the group's actual view, but the data feels hard to argue with.

In workplaces the stakes seem even higher because livelihood is attached to reputation. A professional with RSD may mute their camera to hide a flush of heat after offering an idea. They may speak less in meetings to avoid the risk of public critique. Private messages multiply as they check with one trusted colleague before sending a group reply. The day becomes a long exercise in risk management rather than collaboration.

For students the classroom can be a theatre of threat. Reading aloud can feel like walking a tightrope over a pit. The student looks for the tiniest cue of disapproval from peers or the teacher. When none appears, the mind invents one to explain the knot in the stomach. Lunch breaks, meant for rest, are sometimes spent in bathrooms or libraries to avoid social roulette.

People try many ways to cope. One common pattern is over delivery. If I do more than expected, no one will find fault. This strategy can produce impressive output in the short run. Over time it burns through the body's reserves. Another pattern is self-silencing. If I make no waves, there can be no splashback. This can keep a person safe in the short run. Over time it narrows their life until they barely recognise themselves.

Supporters can help without taking over. A partner who notices the signs of spiralling can offer a gentle reality check in private rather than in front of others. A manager can be explicit about what went well in addition to what needs work, not as a courtesy but as accurate feedback. A teacher can set expectations clearly, then invite questions early, so that students are not left filling gaps with worst case stories.

The Hidden Costs of "Masking"

Masking is the set of habits used to look fine while feeling anything but fine. It is an art learned early by many people with RSD. The aim is to keep belonging secure by sanding off the edges that might look too needy, too intense, or too sensitive. On the surface masking appears to work. The person seems competent, agreeable, even charming. Under the surface the price adds up.

The first price is energy. Holding posture, smoothing tone, measuring words, and smiling on cue all day is like carrying a backpack of bricks while acting as if it is full of feathers. The body keeps score. By late afternoon the smallest hitch in a conversation can feel like a cliff face. There is no energy left to climb it.

The second price is clarity. When a person edits their responses all day to make sure they will not upset anyone, they start to lose track of what they think and want. They can describe what is acceptable in a given room, but they struggle to locate their own view. This does not mean they lack opinions. It means the muscle that brings an inner view to the surface has been overused and is now tired and shaky.

The third price is intimacy. Masking makes relationships look smooth and safe, but it also creates distance. If you rarely show your worry, your partner cannot learn how to meet you there. If you always say, "It is fine," people will stop checking. You will be praised for being easy, and you will feel alone in a crowded house. Many people describe this loneliness as the hardest part of adult life with RSD.

Some people try to pay the masking bill by withdrawing. They reduce contact to reduce risk. This can bring short relief but often costs opportunity. A career stalls. A friendship does not deepen. A creative idea stays in a notebook. Balance is possible, but it is a deliberate practice. It asks for environments that reward clarity and kindness at the same time, and it asks for personal habits that let the mask come off in safe places each day.

Strategies That Help in the Everyday

There is no single technique that dissolves RSD. Daily life becomes easier through a mix of conditions and practices that lower the temperature of social threat and raise the reliability of support. The goal is not perfection. The goal is a day that feels liveable without constant performance or collapse.

Start with predictability. When routines hold, the mind has fewer blanks to fill with worst case stories. Set a stable morning rhythm that includes something small and steady, like stretching while the kettle boils. Keep a simple checklist for departures, because checklists reduce the fear of missing a step and the shame that often follows. Bedtime routines matter as much as morning ones. Sleep is the most democratic therapy we have. It restores the brief space between a cue and a conclusion, and that space is priceless when you live with RSD.

Use language that separates feeling from fact. A short practice is to name the sensation first, then the story. For example, "I feel tight in my chest; my story is that my boss is unhappy with me." The sentence looks simple but it has two parts. The first part welcomes the body's alarm. The second part keeps the mind's theory in quotation marks until there is evidence. People who repeat this practice report that their day includes fewer runaway trains.

Arrange for fast reality checks. Pick one or two trusted people who agree to answer brief clarifying questions when your mind starts to spin. The agreement keeps the request from feeling like a burden. It also reduces the time spent inside guesswork. The goal is not to outsource confidence. The goal is to reduce false alarms before they set off the sprinkler system.

Make feedback safer. If you lead others, create rituals that place affirmation and improvement in the same frame. Say what landed, say what needs work, and say what to do next. Precision builds trust. If you are on the receiving end, ask for examples and next steps. Vague critique is rocket-fuel for RSD. Clear critique is manageable because it points somewhere.

Protect recovery time with the same seriousness you bring to obligations. The nervous system cannot live on a diet of performance. Small islands of restoration prevent the crash and rebuild cycle that many people know too well. Ten minutes of quiet. A walk without a phone. A hobby that brings full attention for a while. These are not side dishes. They are the fuel that keeps the engine from knocking.

Let close people in on the pattern. Explain what spiralling looks like for you and what helps. Some people want reassurance. Others want help checking the story against the facts. Some want a pause and a cup of tea. Be specific, and keep the request small. When supporters know what to do, they can offer help without guessing or lecturing.

Finally, practice warm regard toward yourself. This is not a slogan. It is a decision to treat your pain as real while refusing to let it define your worth. Warm regard sounds like, "This is hard, and I am still allowed to take up space." It chooses steadiness over drama. It forgives the mind for shouting false alarms. It welcomes joy without demanding certainty. Over time, warm regard becomes a tone you carry, and that tone makes daily life less jagged.

Daily life with RSD is an uneven road, but it is a road. People find ways to steer, to slow, to merge, to stop for fuel, and to pick up passengers who make the trip lighter. Progress is sometimes quiet. It looks like attending the meeting and speaking once. It looks like sending the email without five drafts. It looks like going to bed without replaying the day for an hour. These are not small wins. They are the architecture of a life that is no longer built around fear of rejection.

Chap 6: Love, Relationships & RSD

The Promise and the Risk of Intimacy

Love magnifies everything. It is the space where people long to be most fully seen and most fully accepted. For someone living with Rejection Sensitive Dysphoria, this longing carries enormous intensity. The very closeness that makes relationships fulfilling is also what makes them dangerous. No workplace critique, no classroom slight, no passing interaction compares with the weight of a partner's glance, tone, or silence.

Intimacy asks for vulnerability. To love another person is to hand them a set of keys: keys to your mood, your sense of belonging, your stability. When those keys are placed in the hands of someone with RSD, the transaction can feel both exhilarating and terrifying. Exhilarating because closeness offers the possibility of unconditional acceptance. Terrifying because every pause, every unanswered message, every shift in tone can be read as rejection.

In the early stages of a relationship, this dynamic often creates strong highs and lows. The first sign of interest from a partner can feel electrifying. Affection is not merely pleasant — it is proof of worth. On the other hand, any withdrawal, even brief, can feel like a collapse. The body responds as though the entire foundation of the relationship has been threatened, even if the other person was simply distracted or tired.

For the partner of someone with RSD, this can be confusing. They may not understand why a delayed reply leads to visible distress, or why a casual remark is replayed for hours. Without context, they may think their loved one is overreacting or overly needy. In truth, the emotional system of a person with RSD does not measure risk the way others do. For someone with RSD, even a small hint of rejection can feel like an electric shock rather than a passing nudge.

The Cycle of Reassurance and Doubt

One of the central patterns in RSD relationships is the cycle of reassurance and doubt. The person with RSD seeks reassurance, not because they are manipulative or demanding, but because their nervous system interprets small signals as large threats. When reassurance is given, relief is often immediate. But relief is fragile. Doubt creeps back quickly, sometimes within hours, sometimes within minutes.

This cycle can leave both partners exhausted. The one with RSD feels guilty for asking again and again, but unable to silence the alarms without checking. The partner feels worn down, unable to offer reassurance at the pace demanded. If left unspoken, resentment can grow on both sides.

The key to breaking this cycle lies not in withholding reassurance, nor in offering it endlessly, but in creating shared understanding. When a partner knows that the distress is rooted in RSD, not in lack of trust, they can respond with steadier compassion. When the person with RSD learns to label their reactions as part of the condition, not as truth, they can reduce the sense of catastrophe.

Still, the cycle does not vanish. It becomes a pattern to be managed rather than a storm to be feared. Couples who succeed in this often report that communication grows deeper. The very act of naming and negotiating the cycle becomes an exercise in intimacy rather than a failure of it.

Attraction and Fear

Desire in relationships with RSD often comes laced with fear. Wanting someone means opening the door to rejection by them. This can create a paradoxical push-pull dynamic. On one hand, the person may pursue closeness with overwhelming devotion, showering the partner with attention and affection. On the other, they may suddenly withdraw or test the partner, trying to pre-empt rejection by controlling when it happens.

These shifts can bewilder partners. One day they feel cherished beyond measure, the next they sense a wall. Both sides may feel unstable. The person with RSD is not trying to play games. They are trying to manage intolerable levels of risk.

Sexual intimacy carries similar tensions. The vulnerability of physical closeness can make every gesture, every hesitation, every word charged with meaning. A partner rolling to the side after sex can be read as indifference. A moment of distraction can be read as disapproval. The pain is not imaginary — it is experienced in the body with real force. Yet it may be invisible to the partner who meant nothing by their action.

Conflict and the Fear of Abandonment

All couples argue. In relationships touched by RSD, arguments can feel catastrophic. A sharp tone or raised voice does not just signal anger in the moment. It signals the possibility of being discarded. The nervous system leaps to the worst conclusion: the relationship is ending. This is why some individuals with RSD will go to extraordinary lengths to avoid conflict, even at the expense of their own needs.

Avoidance has costs. Needs are suppressed. Resentments grow. The partner may never know what truly matters to their loved one, because the fear of driving them away silences honest expression. The relationship then tilts into imbalance. The partner without RSD becomes the definer of boundaries, while the partner with RSD becomes the keeper of peace at any cost.

Other times, the opposite occurs: conflict leads to explosive reaction. The pain of perceived rejection bursts out as rage, tears, or accusations. These reactions can surprise even the person with RSD, who may later feel shame for their intensity. They did not plan to escalate. Their system registered threat and responded with the equivalent of fire alarms.

In both cases — avoidance or explosion — the common root is fear of abandonment. Recognising this root can help couples step back from the surface drama and see the deeper vulnerability beneath.

When Love Feels Conditional

A difficult pattern in RSD relationships is the sense that love is always conditional. Even when a partner expresses genuine devotion, the person with RSD may struggle to believe it. "They say they love me, but what if I fail tomorrow?" The horizon of security is always close, always about to expire.

This sense of conditionality can drive perfectionism. A person may try to become the flawless partner, anticipating every need, avoiding every mistake. This can look ideal on the surface, but it is not sustainable. It breeds exhaustion and inauthenticity. Over time the partner may feel smothered, or may sense that the relationship is built on anxiety rather than freedom.

The paradox is painful: the person with RSD often gives enormous love, loyalty, and devotion, yet struggles to believe they deserve the same in return. They wait for the shoe to drop, sometimes so intently that they cannot enjoy the floor beneath their feet.

Breaking this pattern involves building trust not just in the partner, but in the durability of love itself. Love must be re-understood as something that can withstand mistakes, disagreements, and imperfect days. For many with RSD, this is a radical concept. It may require therapy, patient communication, and repeated experiences of being accepted even when not perfect.

Patterns from the Past: How Old Wounds Show Up in Love

It's not just the current partner who shows up in a relationship. Every past rejection, every moment of abandonment or humiliation, often walks through the door right alongside the person with RSD. These memories may not be consciously recalled, but they echo in the reactions and assumptions that shape the present.

Someone who was bullied in adolescence may react disproportionately to sarcasm from a partner. Someone who experienced neglect may panic when their messages go unread for a few hours. A past betrayal can make even sincere affection feel like it might be temporary or performative. These reactions often feel "over the top" to the partner but, to the person with RSD, they make perfect emotional sense. They are responses to real pain, just not always the pain of this moment.

The challenge is that these old patterns often get projected onto the current partner. Without meaning to, the person with RSD might assign motives or traits that don't belong. "You're just like everyone else." "You're going to leave eventually." "You think I'm too much." These are not just fears, they are predictions based on a long pattern of pain. And when spoken aloud, they can feel like accusations.

This is where therapy - or at the very least, intentional reflection - can make a huge difference. When someone with RSD begins to distinguish between past pain and present reality, a new level of emotional freedom becomes possible. They begin to recognize when their nervous system is reacting to a ghost, not their partner. And in those moments, they have a choice: not just to react, but to respond.

Partners, too, benefit from understanding these dynamics. It's not about becoming a therapist or walking on eggshells. It's about having the insight to pause and ask: "Is this about now, or is this about then?" That single question can sometimes change the entire shape of a conversation.

Breakups and Their Aftermath

When relationships end, the pain for someone with RSD can be overwhelming. All breakups hurt, but RSD magnifies the loss into something closer to annihilation. The ending confirms every fear: "I was not good enough, I was disposable, I was foolish to believe."

Recovery can take far longer than expected. Ghosting, where someone disappears from communication without explanation, is particularly brutal. It bypasses closure and leaves the person with RSD to fill in the gaps with their worst fears. The absence of clarity often confirms everything the internal critic has ever said: that they're forgettable, annoying, disposable.

These emotional wounds can stay raw for years, especially if there was no opportunity for honest communication at the end.

Even short relationships can leave deep marks, because the person invested fully and felt each moment with heightened intensity. Rumination becomes relentless. Every text, every conversation, every silence is replayed. Shame floods in. The person may vow never to risk love again.

Yet many do try again. Love is too central a human drive to be extinguished by fear. The challenge is to enter new relationships with clearer awareness of how RSD operates. Partners who understand the condition, or who learn about it together, often create safer foundations. The story does not have to end in avoidance. It can end in better preparation.

Building Relationships That Last

For couples where one or both partners live with RSD, longevity depends on a mix of compassion, structure, and realism. Compassion means recognising that reactions are not chosen but experienced. Structure means creating rituals of communication that prevent spirals; such as regular check-ins, explicit expressions of care, and agreed-upon signals for reassurance. Realism means knowing that RSD will not vanish, but can be managed together.

Partners can learn to say, "I love you, and I know your brain is telling you otherwise right now." That sentence separates the person from the reaction without belittling either. The person with RSD can learn to pause before demanding reassurance, naming the feeling as fear rather than as fact. Both can practice forgiveness, because mistakes will happen.

Importantly, joy must not be forgotten. RSD relationships can become dominated by vigilance and repair. Couples need deliberate space for play, laughter, and shared adventure. These moments are not extras, they are the proof that love is larger than fear.

Love, relationships, and RSD will never be a friction-free mix. But neither are they doomed. With shared language, steady compassion, and deliberate effort, couples can build bonds that are not defined by dysphoria, but by resilience. The heartache of RSD remains real, but so does the possibility of enduring love.

Practical Tools for Loving with RSD

Before we close this chapter, it's worth grounding the emotional insight in something tangible. Relationships impacted by RSD benefit enormously from structure, language, and shared agreements. Below are a few of the most effective tools used by individuals and couples navigating this terrain:

1. The Two-Hour Rule

When emotions spike, agree to pause major discussions for at least two hours. This allows each person to regulate, reflect, and re-enter with more clarity. It prevents spiralling conversations that become battles.

2. Written Check-Ins

For those who struggle to say what they feel in the moment, agree to use a shared journal or text log. Prompts like "Today I felt triggered when..." or "What I needed but didn't know how to ask for was..." can bypass defensiveness and allow emotional honesty to emerge in calmer conditions.

3. Signal Words

Agree on non-charged code phrases that mean "I'm dysregulated" or "I need closeness" without requiring long explanations. Something as simple as "I'm blinking red" or "traffic jam" can alert a partner that the inner alarm bells are ringing without blame or escalation.

4. Repair Rituals

Conflict is inevitable. What matters most is the return. Create small, mutual rituals for re-connection after tension or misunderstandings. This could be a short walk, a shared playlist, or five minutes of quiet physical closeness. Rituals help rewire emotional memory, reminding both people that rupture does not equal abandonment.

5. Scheduled Reassurance Windows

Instead of sporadic, panic-driven reassurance seeking, some couples agree on scheduled times for connection and affirmation. For example: "Every night before bed, we'll take 10 minutes to reconnect and talk about anything that's come up." Predictability calms the nervous system, and structure offers relief to both partners.

None of these strategies is a cure. But they are scaffolding. They allow two people to build something stronger than reactive emotion alone: a relationship shaped by intention, empathy, and honest boundaries. These tools don't erase the pain of rejection sensitivity—but they create a container for navigating it together.

And that's the real promise of love with RSD. Not perfection. Not immunity from fear. But connection that holds space for fear, without being consumed by it.

Chap 7: Work, Career & RSD

The weight of professional identity

Work is not only about income. For many people it is the clearest way to answer the question: Who am I in the world? It is where strengths show, where reputation grows, and where belonging is tested in public. When Rejection Sensitive Dysphoria is part of the picture, this arena can feel both promising and perilous. The very structures that allow people to contribute also put them in constant contact with evaluation. That is hard for anyone. It can be relentless for someone whose nervous system treats potential rejection as urgent threat.

The working day is full of tiny judgments. A manager reads a draft. A client delays a reply. A colleague frowns at a meeting agenda. Most of these moments are ambiguous. The ambiguity itself is the problem. Minds that live with RSD often fill gaps with the harshest possible reading. The body follows with racing heart, tight chest, and a flood of self-doubt. None of this means the person is fragile. It means the early warning system is highly tuned to social risk. It fires quickly and it fires often.

Professional identity is built from thousands of such moments. Praise helps. Clear wins help. Still, the nervous system keeps scanning. Many people with RSD describe a feeling of walking across a floor that might give way at any footfall. The fear does not come from vanity. It comes from the simple truth that work determines security and status. The stakes feel large because they are large.

A second layer sits under the fear of error. It is the fear of being judged as a person because of a single imperfect performance. A rough presentation becomes proof of being incompetent. A late email becomes proof of being unreliable. The leap from event to identity is fast. People try to slow it by overpreparing, by polishing every sentence, by reading tone with forensic care. Some succeed for a while. The cost is high.

Learning to live with feedback

Feedback is the grammar of working life. Teams need it to improve. Individuals need it to grow. For people with RSD, the word can land with the force of a verdict. Even measured comments hurt. The sentence that begins with praise and then turns to guidance is heard as a trap. The brain highlights the one part that implies a flaw and fades the rest. The result is not drama. It is a physiological flare that narrows attention to danger.

Annual reviews show the pattern in bright light. Anticipation builds for weeks. Sleep gets lighter. Concentration frays. When the meeting finally arrives, the mind records each suggestion as if it were a public notice of failure. A manager might say, You handled that client well, and next quarter I would like you to prioritise clearer summaries. The person may leave hearing only the last clause. In the evening they replay the phrasing and search for hidden disapproval. The replay can last days.

Avoidance becomes tempting. If feedback hurts, one solution is to step away from situations that trigger it. People delay sharing drafts, ask to skip peer reviews, or accept roles that carry less scrutiny. Another solution is to drown the fear in work. If I deliver flawless output, no one can find fault. That plan works until it does not. Burnout arrives quietly at first, then all at once.

The alternative is not to pretend feedback is painless. It is to build structures that make it tolerable. Managers can learn to be specific, balanced, and directive. Specific means you describe the work precisely. Balanced means you place strengths and changes in the same frame without letting either disappear. Directive means you add a next step so the mind has something to do other than ruminate. People on the receiving end can request this format. It is not coddling. It is good practice for any team.

Colleagues, alliances, and the social web of work

Tasks are the visible part of a job. Relationships are the part that decides whether a day ends with fuel in the tank or with nothing left. For someone with RSD, the social web at work is a constant stream of signals that must be interpreted. A greeting that feels cool, a joke that lands oddly, a missed invitation to coffee. Each small event can grow large in the mind.

Misunderstandings are common. Withdrawal to recover looks like aloofness. Quiet focus looks like disinterest. Checking a message twice before sending looks like indecision. Colleagues cannot see the cost of keeping steady in public. They see only the surface. Over time, the gap between effort and recognition can feel like a private injustice.

Alliances help. One or two trusted colleagues who can give quick reality checks can change the tone of a week. The agreement is simple. When I spiral, I will ask you a short question. When you see me worry about a neutral cue, you will offer a brief, plain, and honest read. In return I will do the same for you. The point is not therapy at the desk. The point is to reduce guesswork and return attention to the work itself.

Belonging is built from predictability. Teams that share information openly limit the empty spaces where harsh stories breed. Clear agendas, explicit expectations, and visible appreciation reduce the need to read tea leaves. None of this is special treatment. It is what healthy workplaces do when they want people to spend energy on the actual mission.

Meetings, messages, and the noise in between

Meetings compress many of the pressures of work into short windows. People watch each other. Ideas are aired. Decisions are made in irregular bursts. For a person with RSD, a meeting can feel like walking into bright light. The mind tracks every raised eyebrow and every shift in the chair. If a contribution is met with silence, the silence can ring in the ears for hours.

Preparation can help, but overpreparation can become another trap. Some people write full scripts for remarks and then feel panic when the meeting flows in a different direction. A more humane approach is to prepare small anchors. What is the single point I want to land. What question can I ask if I lose my footing. What simple summary can I offer at the end if the conversation meanders.

Messages in the digital workplace bring their own patterns. Short replies without greetings, delayed responses outside meeting hours, and threads where others receive reactions while yours sits untouched. The brain supplies a meaning for each of these. Most of those meanings are wrong. One practical habit is to slow the jump from cue to conclusion by adopting a house rule. I will assume neutral intent until evidence says otherwise. It is not a mantra. It is a discipline that preserves energy.

Remote and hybrid work change the picture again. Without the informal cues of a shared space, imagination takes over. Cameras off can mean ten different things. Slack silence can mean fifty. The fix is not constant video. It is explicit rhythms. Teams that set clear norms for response times, meeting cameras, and status messages create air for people who otherwise live in constant doubt about whether they are visible.

Ambition, overwork, and fallow seasons

RSD does not blunt ambition. It can sharpen it. The wish to prove value and to avoid disapproval drives long hours and fine detail. Many high performers live with RSD in secret and build careers on the back of relentless standards. They are often praised as indispensable. The cost is carried at home. Sleep erodes. Relationships thin. Joy drops out of ordinary days. The person begins to experience work as a test that never ends.

On the other end sits avoidance. If you fear the heat of evaluation, you may stand at the door of opportunity and take one step back. You pick roles with less visibility. You decline stretch projects. You keep your ideas to yourself until someone else says them. None of this reflects lack of talent. It reflects a calculation. If I stay small, I stay safe. The price of safety is invisibility.

Between these poles is a path that asks for pacing. Careers are long. They contain seasons for sprinting and seasons for steady miles. People with RSD often need to learn the skill of deliberately choosing the pace, not letting fear choose it for them. That means setting finish lines inside large projects. It means closing the laptop when the work is good enough for today. It means trusting that growth comes from consistency more than from intensity.

After hours: the debrief nobody sees

Work does not end when the clock says so. Many people with RSD carry the day into the evening. They replay the meeting. They edit the email they already sent. They rehearse an apology for a mistake that no one noticed. This private debrief is exhausting. It also feels necessary, because the mind believes that careful review will prevent future pain.

There is a gentler way to end the day. It involves a short, grounded ritual that marks the line between work and home. The steps are plain. Write down the tasks that remain. Choose the first task for tomorrow. Note one piece of feedback for yourself that is both true and kind. Then close the notebook. These actions are small. The effect is not small. The mind has a place to put unfinished business other than the dinner table.

Partners and families can help by understanding that quiet after work is not indifference. It is recovery. Ten minutes alone may be the difference between a tense evening and an ordinary one. When loved ones know this pattern, they can give space without feeling pushed away. When the person with RSD names the need without apology, they reduce confusion and guilt on both sides.

Boundaries, disclosure, and asking for what helps

Boundaries are easy to admire and hard to practice. In the workplace they protect focus and health. For someone with RSD, boundaries also protect dignity. They keep panic from making promises that cannot be met. They keep fear from saying yes to every task. A boundary can be as simple as turning off notifications after a set time or as specific as refusing to take on work that belongs to another role. Clear boundaries invite respect. Vague ones invite negotiation you do not have energy for.

Disclosure is a separate question. Some people choose to tell a manager about RSD. Others do not. There is no single right choice. The decision depends on trust, culture, and personal preference. If you do share, keep it brief and professional. Describe the practical impacts and the supports that help. For example, I thrive with clear written expectations and scheduled check ins. I struggle when tasks arrive without context. What helps me is a quick alignment on scope. This is not a confession. It is a work agreement.

Asking for what helps is easier when you know what helps. That requires observation. Which parts of the day drain you fastest. Which meetings leave you steady rather than shaken. Which forms of feedback you absorb without spiralling. The answers are a map. You can then ask for small adjustments that fit the map. You are not asking for special rules. You are aligning the environment with the way your nervous system operates.

Changing roles and careers without shame

Careers are not straight lines. People change direction for reasons that range from family needs to curiosity to health. RSD can make change feel like failure even when it is wise. A promotion that looks good on paper may come with levels of scrutiny that are not worth the cost. A lateral move might feel like retreat. In truth it may be a strategic shift toward a culture where you can breathe.

Job searches bring the rawest exposure to evaluation. Applications disappear into silence. Interviews hinge on first impressions. Rejections arrive in form letters. The process is designed to be efficient, not humane. People with RSD can protect themselves by setting routines that make the search a job with set hours rather than an open wound.

Send a set number of applications. Build in rest days. Debrief interviews with a trusted person who can separate signal from noise.

Networking is often advised and often dreaded. Treat it as relationship building rather than performance. Ask real questions. Offer help where you can. Follow up once and then let go. If someone goes quiet, assume life got busy. Assume neutrality until proven otherwise. This stance is not naive. It is a way to remain in motion without turning each silence into a story about your worth.

Building the muscle for steady growth

Skills make fear easier to live with. The aim is not to remove sensitivity. It is to build capacity around it. Three areas repay effort.

First, the skill of framing. Before a high-stakes moment, write a tiny brief for yourself. What is the purpose of this task. What result would count as a solid outcome today. What is not in scope. Framing limits the flood of self-blame that arrives when you try to be everything at once.

Second, the skill of repair. You will miss notes. Everyone does. When you do, move to repair rather than rumination. That sounds like this. Thank you for the note. I see what I missed. I will correct the figure and resend by end of day. The sentence does not hide the mistake. It also does not hand your identity over to it. Over time, that habit changes the way your nervous system reads errors. They become events, not definitions.

Third, the skill of celebration. Many people with RSD treat success as a brief pass that will be revoked at the next review. This habit steals motivation. Mark wins in plain ways. Share good news with one ally. Keep a record of outcomes that were recognised by others. On difficult days you will need to borrow confidence from your own archives.

Short portraits

Elena is a nurse in an emergency department. She is trusted by her peers and sought out by families who want clear explanations. She also goes home most nights convinced she missed something that will hurt someone. Her shift ends at midnight, but her head stays in the ward until two. A senior nurse noticed. They now do a two-minute end of shift debrief. What went well. What needs follow up. What can wait for day staff. Elena sleeps sooner. The work is unchanged. The container is different.

Kane is a project manager in a tech firm. He under talks in meetings because he fears saying something that will not land. His written plans are excellent. His spoken presence is faint. A mentor helped him choose one sentence to say in each meeting. State the goal at the start or summarise the next step at the end. Kane can do that without shaking. After six months people describe him as clear and steady. He did not change his personality. He changed his focus.

A steady way to close the workday

No job can remove uncertainty. What you can remove is the sense that you must hold the whole organisation together with your vigilance. A steady close to the day is a practice, not a trick. It may look like this. Choose a sentence that captures the most useful thing you did today. Choose one thing you could do a little better tomorrow and write it as a single action. Then leave your desk as if the work will still be there in the morning, because it will. This is not a slogan. It is a boundary that respects both the job and the person doing it.

Professional life with RSD will always ask for more care in the way feedback is given and received, more patience in the way relationships grow, and more attention to pacing. Those are not weaknesses. They are the conditions under which real contribution becomes possible. Many people build sturdy and satisfying careers once they stop aiming for invulnerability and start building reliability. Stability is not the absence of feeling. It is the presence of habits that carry you through days that are loud with evaluation.

The goal is not a fearless worker. The goal is a life where fear does not run the schedule. That life is built one steady email, one honest check in, and one humane review at a time. It is built in teams that prize clarity over theatre. It is built in bodies that have learned the difference between a cue and a conclusion. Over years, the same sensitivity that once felt like a liability can sharpen attention to people and detail in ways that organisations value. When that attention is paired with pacing and support, it becomes an asset that lasts.

Chap 8: RSD in Children and Teenagers

Early Signs at Home

Rejection Sensitive Dysphoria often shows itself long before a child has the language to name it. Parents may notice that their son or daughter reacts more strongly to disappointment than peers. What looks like a small correction can provoke tears, withdrawal, or even anger. A remark such as "tidy your room" might land not as a neutral instruction but as evidence of failure. When an older sibling sighs in impatience, the younger child might vanish to their room, convinced they have let the family down.

In many cases, the intensity of the child's response seems out of proportion to the event. A dropped toy leads to sobbing. A small scolding is replayed endlessly in their minds. These are not simply moments of immaturity. For some children they are signs of a nervous system that experiences disapproval as threat.

The home environment can both soften and intensify this sensitivity. Parents who respond with warmth, patience, and predictable boundaries often see their child recover more quickly. A calm voice or a hug can help the child regulate again. By contrast, if parents react harshly or inconsistently, the child's fear of rejection deepens. Families may notice cycles of clinginess followed by withdrawal: the child seeks reassurance, then hides out of guilt for needing too much.

Distinguishing between ordinary childhood sensitivity and the deeper patterns of RSD is not always easy. All children crave approval. All feel stung by criticism. But when the sting is overwhelming, lingers far beyond the moment, and begins to shape avoidance of everyday activities, parents are right to look more closely.

School as a Stage of Constant Evaluation

For many children, school is where RSD first becomes undeniable. Classrooms are structured around evaluation: grades, feedback, peer comparison, competition. For most children these are challenges. For a child with RSD, they can feel like daily verdicts on their worth.

Imagine the simple act of raising a hand in class. For one child it is a moment of engagement. For another it is a calculated risk. If the answer is right, relief is brief. If the answer is wrong, shame burns for hours, sometimes days. Even neutral teacher responses may be misread. "Good try" can feel like polite failure.

Peer dynamics intensify the strain. A classmate who does not return a smile, a group that laughs together without them, or a partner who chooses someone else for a project: each is absorbed as evidence of exclusion. Teachers may not notice, because these reactions are internalised. Outwardly the child may comply and stay quiet. Inside, they may be carrying crushing self-doubt.

Some cope by overachieving. They stay up late to perfect homework, chase top grades, and seek constant approval. Others cope by disappearing, drifting to the back of the room, avoiding participation altogether. Both strategies have costs: exhaustion on one side, invisibility on the other.

Friendships and Social Challenges

Friendship is one of the defining features of childhood and adolescence. Even without RSD, relationships at this age can be fragile, shifting, and sometimes bewildering. A child might be inseparable from a friend one week and feel excluded the next. For those with RSD, the stakes are even higher. Small social shifts can feel like major ruptures.

Consider a child who discovers their best friend has sat with someone else at lunch. To many children this is a mild disappointment. For a child with RSD, it can feel like betrayal or abandonment. Similarly, a message that goes unanswered or a laugh that is not shared can be interpreted as proof of rejection. What others shrug off, they carry as evidence that they do not belong.

During adolescence, this sensitivity is amplified by the constant presence of social media and digital interaction. A group chat that continues without them, a post where they are not tagged, or an online game where friends do not invite them can spark hours of ruminating. To parents, these reactions can seem excessive, but for the teenager with RSD, digital signals are treated as hard evidence. They are already primed to connect self-worth with acceptance, and the internet magnifies every cue.

Conflicts with friends are often remembered in detail. A sharp comment is not quickly forgotten. Even after an apology, the teen may replay the moment, feeling the pain again and again. Over time, this can lead them to hold back from forming new friendships. Outwardly they may appear shy, aloof, or even indifferent. Inwardly they long for connection but fear rejection too much to risk it.

Adults can help by normalising the ebb and flow of friendship. Explaining that disagreements are common and repair is possible provides perspective. Simple role-play of apologies and reconciliations can give children scripts to fall back on when emotions are high. When adults model forgiveness and repair in their own relationships, children observe that conflict need not mean the end of a bond.

Family Dynamics and the Adolescent Push and Pull

The teenage years are a dance between independence and dependence. For teenagers with RSD, this natural push and pull with parents and family is often heightened. They may seek autonomy, demanding privacy and freedom. Moments later they may crave reassurance, collapsing into tears after a minor setback. Parents can feel whiplash, unsure whether to step closer or stand back.

Siblings add another layer of complexity. Praise directed at one child can be heard as condemnation of another. Even casual comparisons, such as "your brother finds maths easy," may wound deeply. Family meals or conversations that seem routine can be remembered by the teen as moments of humiliation. Parents sometimes describe walking on eggshells, never knowing what remark will be misinterpreted.

The truth is that the teen is not deliberately manipulative. Their nervous system is primed to treat even small signs of disapproval as danger. Understanding this allows families to respond with steadiness rather than overreaction. Clear expectations, predictable routines, and consistent reassurance can help reduce the child's sense of chaos.

Compassion, however, does not mean removing all challenges. Shielding a teen from criticism or consequence leaves them unprepared for adult life. The balance lies in offering both safety and growth. Parents who maintain structure while providing warmth often find that their teen becomes more willing to risk participation. They learn that mistakes will not cost them love or belonging.

Self-Image and the Teenage Mirror

Adolescence always brings new intensity to self-perception. Bodies change, social hierarchies shift, and identity questions rise to the surface. For teenagers with RSD, these changes can feel overwhelming. They may scrutinise themselves harshly in the mirror, convinced that every perceived flaw is visible to the world.

The need for social acceptance magnifies these insecurities. A laugh overheard in a hallway may be interpreted as ridicule. A peer's compliment might be dismissed as pity. Romantic interest is particularly loaded. A crush who does not reciprocate can trigger despair. A cancelled plan may feel like public humiliation.

School events also take on greater weight. A stumble on stage during a play, a missed note in a concert, or a mistake in a sports match can replay endlessly in their mind. Long after others have forgotten, the teen continues to relive the moment. These experiences shape self-esteem in ways that can carry into adulthood.

Support at this stage must emphasise perspective. Teens need help separating event from identity. A failed test is not evidence of stupidity. A cancelled date is not proof of worthlessness. Parents and teachers who reinforce these distinctions repeatedly help to build an inner voice that counters the harsh judgments of RSD. Over time, this repetition plants seeds of resilience.

Bullying and Exclusion

Bullying is painful for any child, but for those with RSD it can be devastating. Teasing, exclusion, or criticism is not just unpleasant. It is experienced as deep confirmation of the fear that they are unworthy or unlovable.

Bullying can be obvious: name-calling, mocking, or physical aggression. But it is often subtle. A group that quietly leaves them out of an invitation. A friend who suddenly ignores them in the hallway. A rolling of eyes from a peer when they speak in class. These moments may not even be noticed by adults, but to the child with RSD, they leave scars.

The digital world has added new dimensions. Online bullying can happen around the clock, and the permanence of written or shared content intensifies the hurt. A cruel comment in a group chat, a photo shared without consent, or a sarcastic caption on social media can replay endlessly. Unlike spoken words, which fade, online posts can be revisited and reinterpreted over and over.

Children with RSD are particularly vulnerable because they are already primed to interpret cues as rejection. What others might dismiss as a joke can feel like unbearable humiliation. What others may shrug off as ordinary teasing can lead to weeks of avoidance or depression.

Intervention is critical. Parents and teachers must take even mild forms of bullying seriously. Encouraging bystanders to speak up, teaching empathy in classrooms, and creating safe reporting systems can protect vulnerable children. When bullying occurs, immediate support helps prevent the child from embedding it as evidence of lifelong rejection.

Parent–School Partnership

Children with RSD thrive best when the adults in their lives work together. Parents bring intimate knowledge of their child's triggers and strengths. Teachers bring insight into classroom dynamics. When these perspectives are shared, children benefit.

Too often, children with RSD are misunderstood at school. Their quiet withdrawal may be mistaken for disengagement. Their perfectionism may be praised, even as it drains them. Their outbursts may be labelled as misbehaviour rather than distress. Without context, teachers may discipline rather than support.

Parents can help by opening conversations early. Explaining that their child is highly sensitive to rejection and feedback allows teachers to respond with compassion. Specific strategies can be agreed on: phrasing corrections gently, praising effort as much as outcome, and offering opportunities for repair after mistakes.

In some countries, formal supports such as IEPs or 504 plans (in the US) can include accommodations for emotional regulation. Even without formal plans, many schools are willing to adapt when given clear information. Examples include allowing private feedback instead of public corrections, offering flexible ways to participate, or pairing the child with supportive peers.

When schools listen, children learn that support is possible outside the home. When parents advocate calmly and consistently, children learn that they are not alone in navigating their challenges. This partnership does not remove sensitivity, but it does create a safer environment in which the child can grow.

Building Resilience and Hope

Living with RSD as a child or teenager is undeniably hard. Sensitivity shapes daily experiences and can make ordinary events feel overwhelming. Yet with the right support, these years can also be a time of growth. The goal is not to eliminate sensitivity but to give it safe outlets and constructive direction.

One of the strongest protective factors is validation. When children hear that their feelings are real and understandable, they are more likely to learn how to manage them. Dismissing reactions as "too much" or "dramatic" teaches shame. By contrast, saying, "I can see that hurt you more than it might hurt someone else" acknowledges the reality of their experience while keeping the door open to recovery.

Another factor is modelling. Children watch how adults handle rejection, conflict, and mistakes. A parent who admits, "I felt embarrassed when I made that error, but I reminded myself everyone makes mistakes," offers a powerful lesson. A teacher who apologises after snapping at a student shows that repair is possible. These examples are more effective than any lecture.

Therapy can play a role, particularly cognitive-behavioural approaches that help children test automatic thoughts. If a teenager insists, "No one likes me," a therapist may guide them to examine the evidence and consider alternative explanations. Over time, this practice helps them challenge the reflex of self-condemnation.

Peer support is also invaluable. Meeting others who share similar sensitivities reduces the sense of being abnormal or alone. Group therapy, youth clubs with a focus on inclusion, or even online communities can offer safe spaces. The simple act of hearing "me too" often reduces shame.

Families and schools can deliberately create opportunities for safe failure. Children need to experience that mistakes, while painful, are survivable. A lost game, a forgotten line in a play, or a poor grade should be framed as moments to learn rather than verdicts on character. Over time, the nervous system learns that rejection or failure does not equal annihilation.

It is equally important to highlight the strengths that sensitivity can bring. Children and teens with RSD often have heightened empathy. They notice when others are hurting. They may excel in creative fields where emotional intensity is an advantage. They often form deep, loyal bonds once they feel secure. Pointing out these qualities helps build pride rather than shame.

Adolescence is also a time when young people begin to explore identity and meaning. For teenagers with RSD, guiding them toward activities that channel sensitivity - such as art, writing, volunteering, or mentoring younger children - can create a sense of purpose. When sensitivity becomes a tool for connection rather than a burden, hope grows.

Above all, the message must be consistent: rejection is painful, but it is survivable. Children and teenagers with RSD need repeated experiences of making mistakes, repairing relationships, and moving forward. Each success rewires their expectations, teaching them that pain does not mean the end of love or belonging.

Preparing for Adulthood

As children with RSD move through adolescence, the focus gradually shifts from protection to preparation. The world beyond school and home will not always understand their sensitivities. Criticism will come, friendships will falter, and rejection will occur in relationships, studies, and work. Shielding them entirely would leave them vulnerable when they step into adult life.

The task of parents, teachers, and caregivers is therefore twofold: to provide enough safety for recovery and enough challenge for growth. This balance is never perfect. Some days will tilt too far toward protection, others toward challenge. What matters most is consistency. Children who trust that the adults in their lives are not going to abandon them learn to take risks they once avoided.

Adolescence also brings opportunities to experiment with independence. A teenager with RSD may resist taking these steps at first, fearing failure. Gentle encouragement - signing up for a club, trying a part-time job, joining a sports team - can expand their sense of possibility. With each attempt, successful or not, the young person gathers evidence that they can survive outside the protective bubble.

Parents sometimes ask whether their child will ever "grow out" of RSD. The truth is that sensitivity is a lifelong trait. What changes is how it is managed. A teenager who learns coping skills, builds resilience, and experiences repair will carry those tools into adulthood. They may still feel pain more sharply than others, but they will not be defined by it.

Closing Reflections

RSD in childhood and adolescence is not a passing phase. It shapes self-image, friendships, school experiences, and family relationships. Left unsupported, it can cast long shadows. But with understanding, structure, and compassion, those same years can build resilience.

Children and teenagers with RSD are not broken. They are navigating a nervous system that reacts differently, one that interprets rejection as threat. When the adults around them respond with steadiness and belief, the child learns that sensitivity can coexist with strength. The very qualities that make life difficult - empathy, intensity, loyalty - can become gifts when guided well.

The message to carry forward is simple: rejection will hurt, but it is survivable. With practice, perspective, and support, children and teenagers with RSD can grow into adults who live full lives, sensitive yet strong, and able to use their depth of feeling to enrich both their own lives and the lives of others.

Chap 9: Managing the Emotional Storm

The shape of the storm

People who live with RSD often describe sudden emotional weather. One moment is ordinary. The next is charged with heat, pressure, and noise. The trigger might be small in the eyes of others. A short reply. A face that looks impatient. A pause where a kind word should have arrived. The inner shift is not small. The body responds as if a loud alarm just sounded in a crowded room.

The first signs are physical. The heart speeds up. Breathing becomes shallow. The muscles around the neck and shoulders tighten as if bracing for impact. Some feel a flush in the face or a hollow in the stomach. Others feel a fog, as if it is suddenly hard to think in complete sentences. The mind, trying to make sense of these changes, grabs the nearest story that explains them. It picks the story it has practiced for years. I am being rejected. I am about to lose my place. I am in trouble.

The story and the body reinforce one another. Sensations feed thoughts. Thoughts fuel sensations. Soon the whole field of attention narrows to the trigger. People say, I could not think of anything else for hours. This is not drama. It is a predictable loop between physiology and interpretation. Understanding that loop is not the same as excusing the fallout. It is the starting point for managing it.

Storms vary in length and intensity. Some pass in minutes with a long exhale and a return to baseline. Others swell and break again and again across a whole day. The longer storms usually include rumination. The person replays words, facial expressions, and small choices. They try to find the precise moment where things went wrong. The search is tireless and usually fruitless. It leaves the person drained and, often, ashamed.

Shame complicates recovery. After the surge, people often tell themselves that they should have known better, should have stayed calm, should have been immune. That tone of self talk keeps the body on alert and makes the next storm more likely. A more accurate view is that storms are part of how this nervous system handles social threat. The task is not to pretend the weather is fine. The task is to detect early patterns, ride out the worst of the surge without damaging acts, and shorten the aftershock.

Why storms start so fast

Speed is the feature that unsettles people most. The shift from steady to flooded can take seconds. The reason sits in basic brain design. Signals that hint at social exclusion are processed quickly and with priority. Evolution made that choice long before any of us were born. Groups conferred safety. Losing the group was risky. The body still treats a hint of exclusion as urgent.

For many with RSD, past episodes of rejection sit close to the surface. They are stored as vivid memories. When a new cue appears, those memories light up and add weight. A late reply brings back the evenings of being ignored. A teacher's sigh unlocks the memory of a public correction years ago. The present becomes layered with the past, so the reaction belongs to both. This does not mean the person is living in the past. It means the past is contributing force to the present reaction.

Another reason storms start fast is that people often run at a baseline of tension. Days spent watching for signs of disapproval build a background hum that is already high. When the hum is high, even a small input pushes the system into overload. Sleep loss, hunger, and long periods without rest increase this effect. None of these causes are mysterious. They are practical and, crucially, modifiable.

Speed cannot be removed entirely. It can be slowed. People learn to insert small, reliable actions at the first hint of surge. Those actions are not deep philosophies. They are simple, physical anchors that give the thinking parts of the brain time to return to the conversation.

Early warning signs you can trust

Most storms give a little notice. The notice might be brief, but it is there. Some feel a change in temperature in the face or hands. Some notice a jump in volume inside the chest. Some hear a line in the mind that always appears first, like a title card. For example, Here we go, or Of course, or They never cared. Others see behaviour cues. The fingers fly to the phone. The cursor hovers over a message. The jaw sets.

It helps to make a private list of two or three early signs that show up most often. Keep the list small. A long inventory is hard to remember in a rush. The goal is quick recognition. Once you name a sign, you can pair it with a next step. For instance, When I notice the jump in my chest, I stand up and take three slow breaths. When the title card appears, I look at one object in the room and describe it to myself. When my hand reaches for the phone, I pause and put it screen down for one minute.

These steps sound too simple because they are simple. Simplicity is a feature. The middle of a surge is no time for a complex plan. You want short, repeatable moves that slightly widen attention and invite your thinking mind to rejoin the scene. If you repeat them often, they become habits that run before the spiral takes full hold.

Interrupting the surge without making it worse

Early interruption prevents a narrow, hot moment from becoming a wide, long one. The art is to choose actions that reduce fuel rather than add it. Two domains matter most at first: body and language.

Body first. Slow the exhale. A pattern many people use is in for four, out for six. Lengthening the out breath engages the part of the nervous system that eases the alarm. If counting is hard, choose a steady visual instead. Look at the corner of a frame, the edge of a book, or the line where the floor meets the wall. Hold attention there for three full breaths. If you can safely move, change posture. Stand if you were sitting. Sit if you were standing. Roll your shoulders. Release the jaw. Movement tells the body that you are not trapped.

Language second. Words shape what the body does next. Swap certainty for curiosity. Replace "They hate me" with "I feel unwanted and I do not yet know why." Replace "I ruined everything" with "I made a choice I do not like and I can still make another one." This is not positive thinking. It is accurate thinking. It holds the feeling and it holds the unknown at the same time.

Behavior third. Do less, not more. The impulse in a storm is to fire off messages, confront, defend, or fix. Most damage in RSD storms comes from actions taken at peak intensity. If you can, set a short boundary with others. "I need a moment. I will come back to this in ten minutes." If that is not possible, set a boundary with yourself. "No messages for five minutes." The gap is small. It is also large enough to keep you from creating a second problem on top of the first.

Communicating during a storm

Storms happen in relationships, so communication matters. People cannot read your nervous system from the outside. Let them in with a simple, agreed phrase. Couples and close friends often use, "I am storming." Teams sometimes use, "I need a short pause." The phrase is not an excuse to withdraw forever. It is a signal that you are working to stay constructive.

Tone matters during a surge. Keep sentences short and literal. Avoid questions that sound like accusations. Avoid interpretations of the other person's motives. Focus on what you will do. "I am going to get a glass of water. I will be back in five minutes." Or, "I want to finish this, and I need a moment to calm down."

If you are on the other side, give space without leaving. Say one or two sentences that demonstrate steadiness. "I am here. Take your time." Or, "We will pick this up when you are ready." Then hold that line. Do not press for quick resolution if the person is not yet able to think clearly. Quick resolution reached through pressure is unstable and will not last.

The digital storm

Phones and laptops create their own weather. The storm that begins with a read receipt and no reply is familiar to many. The tools that help in physical space also help here, but we need a few additions.

Set house rules for reading and responding. Some people choose not to open messages during times when they cannot reply. Others create a rule that they will not interpret tone from short texts. Teams can agree to norms that reduce ambiguity. For instance, adding a short, clear acknowledgment when a message is received and will be answered later. These practices are not about coddling. They are about keeping work and relationships from becoming hostage to guesswork.

Unfollow or mute accounts that repeatedly trigger spirals. Curate news and social feeds with a view to your nervous system, not just your interests. If a thread is heated, stand up before responding. If the platform offers a draft or delay feature, use it. The minute you give yourself may prevent a public exchange that prolongs the storm for days.

Riding out the middle

Despite best efforts, some storms peak. When you are at full intensity, the key is to choose containment over explanation. You do not need to win the argument inside your head while your body is in revolt. You need to keep yourself and others safe and avoid actions that will expand the fallout.

Containment looks like this. Reduce stimulation. Turn down lights or step into a quieter space if you can. Lower the volume in the room or in your ears. If music helps, pick something steady and familiar. If you are at work, excuse yourself to the bathroom or a hallway. If you are at home, move to a place where you can breathe without interruption.

Avoid substances that intensify the state. Caffeine, alcohol, and sugar often make the surge sharper. Choose water. If you can eat, choose something plain. This is not a lifestyle lecture. It is a narrow recommendation for a narrow window.

If tears come, let them come. If you need to sit, sit. If you need to pace, pace. Keep your movements slow and safe. Bring attention to contact points. Feel your feet in your shoes. Feel the chair support your weight. The mind can stay noisy while attention rests briefly in the body. That small split gives the surge somewhere to go.

If you must keep engaging with someone while storming, buy time by asking clarifying questions rather than making claims. "Can you repeat the last part." "What would you like me to do next." Short questions keep the exchange moving without adding fuel. They also signal that you are trying to stay present.

After the storm: repair and recovery

Once the surge passes, there is a window for recovery and, later, learning. Do not rush analysis. People love to explain what happened as proof that it will never happen again. Explanations made too soon tend to be harsh and inaccurate. Give yourself a little distance first.

Recovery begins with basics. Drink water. Wash your face. Step outside if weather allows. If you can sleep, sleep. If you cannot sleep, choose a simple, absorbing task for a short period. Fold laundry. Wash dishes. Walk around the block. This is not avoidance. It is the nervous system returning to a manageable state so that thinking can resume.

When you do reflect, keep the lens practical. Ask three questions. What was the first reliable sign that the surge was coming. Which action helped most to keep the peak from getting higher. Is there any repair I owe to someone else now that I have more clarity. Write brief answers. If repair is needed, keep it plain. "I was overwhelmed. I am calmer now. I am sorry for my tone. Here is what I propose next." Do not overexplain. You are rebuilding trust with steadiness, not with pages of text.

Building a personal storm plan

A plan does not need to be elaborate. The best ones fit on a small card or a phone note. Four lines are enough.

1. My early signs: list two or three.
2. My anchors: list two body steps and one language step.
3. My pause rule: define how long you will wait before sending messages or making decisions.
4. My repair script: write two sentences you can use when you return.

The plan is not a promise to be perfect. It is a tool to reduce damage and shorten recovery. Share it with one supportive person if you want an ally. Ask them to remind you of it when you forget you have it.

Prevention that actually helps

Prevention is not a single technique. It is a cluster of ordinary habits that lower baseline tension so that small triggers do not tip you over as easily. None of these are dramatic. The evidence sits in how your days feel over time.

Sleep and rhythm. Regular sleep schedules act like shock absorbers. Even one extra hour across a week can change the intensity of storms. If sleep is hard, treat wind-down as part of work. Dim lights earlier. Stop scrolling earlier. Keep the phone out of arm's reach in bed if possible.

Food and hydration. Stable blood sugar reduces spikes in irritability and anxiety. Keep snacks that you tolerate well available. Drink water before long meetings and before difficult conversations. Small inputs matter to a body that is already watching for threat.

Movement. You do not need heroic workouts. Ten minutes of walking, stretching, or light strength work most days changes how fast your body returns to baseline. Many find that morning movement is best because it sets the tone for the day.

Boundaries. Decide in advance which hours are off limits for reading potentially upsetting messages. Decide which topics you will not debate late at night. Decide how many commitments you will accept in a week. Boundaries are not walls. They are agreements that protect the nervous system from overload.

Connection. Regular contact with one or two people who know your patterns acts like a pressure valve. Do not save all contact for crises. Light, pleasant contact between storms keeps support alive and prevents isolation from growing.

When storms point to larger risks

Most RSD storms are painful but safe. Sometimes they are part of a wider picture that needs more help. If you notice that storms are leading to self harm, to thoughts of not wanting to be alive, or to actions that place you or others at risk, that is a signal to involve professionals. Immediate support from local crisis services, primary care, or mental health services is appropriate in those cases. Safety comes first, then learning.

Some people find that therapy aimed at emotion regulation gives them lifelong tools. Others benefit from skills groups that teach simple practices in a supportive setting. We will discuss medication and medical support later in the book. For this chapter, it is enough to say that help exists, and seeking it is a practical response to a tough problem, not a personal failure.

Two short portraits

Maya, age 28. A colleague forgot to copy her on a client email. She found out when the client replied to everyone else. The surge was instant. She wanted to demand an explanation. Instead she stood up, walked to the kitchen, and counted ten slow breaths while looking at the edge of a cupboard door. She sent a short, steady message asking to be added and offering the figure the team needed. Later she told the colleague what had happened and asked for a quick check on future threads. The relationship stayed intact. The feeling still hurt, but it did not run the day.

Leo, age 16. A friend posted photos from a party he could not attend. He read the lack of a tag as proof that he was out. He felt heat in his face and a drop in his stomach. He put the phone face down and went outside to shoot baskets for fifteen minutes. When he came back, he saw a direct message asking where he had been and saying he was missed. He still felt tender, but the storm had passed enough to read the message as care rather than pity.

A steadier view of storms

Storms are part of the landscape for many who live with RSD. That fact can feel heavy. It can also become less frightening when you have names for early signs, a small set of actions that reduce harm, and a simple plan for repair. People who practice these skills do not become unfeeling. They become better pilots in rough weather.

The point of these practices is not to earn worthiness. You do not have to perform calm to deserve belonging. The point is to protect your days, your relationships, and your work from the worst effects of rapid surges. Over time, storms change character. They still arrive, but they are less likely to sweep away hours of your life. They are less likely to leave behind damage that needs long repair.

When you think about progress, look for quiet signs. You asked for a pause before replying. You slept rather than rewriting a message at two in the morning. You owned a sharp tone and repaired it the next day. These are not small. They are the architecture of stability.

Chap 10: Therapeutic Tools: Mindfulness & More

The case for tools

People living with RSD often know the terrain of their pain in detail. They can describe the quick rise of heat in the chest, the way thoughts rush to conclusions, and the long aftermath of self-blame that follows even small social cues. What is less familiar is a practical set of methods to create space in those moments. A method does not change temperament, and it does not make a sensitive person less human. It gives the person more choice. That is the promise of therapeutic tools. They shift the experience from being carried by the storm to having a hand on the tiller, even when the sea is rough.

A good tool for RSD has three qualities. It is simple enough to use under stress, it is repeatable in different settings, and it supports repair as well as prevention. Simplicity matters because storms move fast. Repeatability matters because the same person must carry the method from kitchen table to classroom to office. Repair matters because even with skill, ruptures will happen, and relationships need a dependable way to mend without weeks of rumination.

Scepticism is common. Many people say they tried deep breathing once and it did not help, or they downloaded a mindfulness app and stopped after three days. That response makes sense. A single attempt rarely changes a habit that has been reinforced by years of threat learning. These tools work like physical training. Small, regular practice grows capacity. When a storm comes, the body reaches for what it has rehearsed. If there has been no rehearsal, a list of techniques will not help. If there has been modest, steady rehearsal, even one or two moves can lower the volume of the surge enough to allow a wiser response.

Think of tools as components in a kit rather than a single solution. Not every tool suits every person, and not every tool suits the same person in every setting. Some days call for breath and grounding. Some days call for a short script to buy time in a tense conversation. Some days need the more deliberate work of testing a harsh thought against facts. The aim of this chapter is to map the options, explain why they are useful, and show how to weave them into a life rather than visiting them only in emergencies.

Culture, values, and context also matter. A student in a noisy house will need different routines than a lawyer in a quiet office. A parent of young children will choose brief, portable practices. A shift worker will anchor tools around changing hours. None of this means the person is less committed. It means the tools are being fitted to the life they must serve. That is how tools become reliable rather than ornamental.

Finally, a word about language. People with RSD often absorb years of messages that call their sensitivity weakness. Tools must not become another way to pass judgment. The goal is not to perform calm to please others. The goal is to reduce harm to the self and to relationships, and to expand the parts of life that bring meaning. When a method serves that goal, it is worth keeping. When it does not, it can be let go.

Mindfulness as attention training

Mindfulness is often presented as serenity on a cushion. In clinical use it is closer to attention training. The practice asks a person to notice the present moment with deliberate focus and with a gentle stance toward whatever appears. That stance is not soft sentiment. It is a practical way to reduce the usual chain that runs from sensation to story to action in a few heartbeats.

People with RSD spend much of the day in two places at once. The body is in the present. The mind is replaying a look from this morning, or predicting a slight that might arrive tomorrow. Mindfulness interrupts this split by giving attention a simple job. Feel the feet on the floor. Track the breath for ten cycles. Listen to the nearest sound and label it as sound rather than meaning. Each time the mind runs off to a grievance or a fear, the instruction is to notice that drift and return. The return is the repetition that changes the skill.

Short practices are enough to begin. Two minutes at breakfast. Three minutes before opening the inbox. Five minutes before sleep. People who keep it brief at first tend to continue. Over weeks the tone of the day shifts. There are still storms, but they are less likely to swallow the next hour. There is a little more space to choose a response rather than being thrown into one. The person is learning how to leave a thought alone when it is not helpful, which is one of the most valuable skills for anyone with RSD.

For those who do not want formal practice, informal moments count. Stand at the sink and feel the temperature of the water. Sit in a meeting and notice breath at the base of the throat for three cycles before speaking. Wait at a red light and let the eyes rest on one object without commentary. These tiny acts are not decoration. They build the muscle of attention so that when pain rises, attention does not vanish completely.

Mindfulness is not moral virtue, and it is not an identity. It is a tool. If a person enjoys group classes, they can use them. If they prefer privacy, a two-minute timer on a phone works just as well. What matters is not the brand of practice but the regular return to the present with a stance of curiosity rather than condemnation. That stance changes what is possible in the next difficult conversation.

Breath as a direct regulator

When the body races, breath follows. Because breathing and the nervous system are tightly linked, breath can be used as a lever to slow the alarm. The most useful patterns are plain. Inhale through the nose, exhale slowly through the mouth. Aim for a longer out breath than in breath. A simple count is four on the inhale and six on the exhale. If counting feels distracting, imagine fogging a mirror on the out breath. The soft sound and longer release help the body register safety.

Another steady method is box breathing. Inhale for four counts, hold for four, exhale for four, hold for four, then repeat. The shape is easy to remember, and the pauses create a sense of edges around the breath. Some prefer 4–7–8 breathing at night. Inhale for four, hold for seven, exhale for eight. The extended exhale promotes drowsiness for people who carry storms into bedtime.

Practice when calm is the rule that turns breath into a reliable tool under stress. A person who only tries slow breathing in the middle of an argument will decide it does not work. A person who rehearses twice a day for a week will notice that their body finds the pattern faster when they need it. The skill is not intellectual. It is physical learning.

Breath pairs well with a brief cue in language. On the inhale, quietly name the feeling. On the exhale, quietly state the intention. In for "hurt," out for "steady." In for "fear," out for "wait." The words are not magic. They keep the mind from spinning while the body rights itself. Together, breath and language turn a runaway moment into a pause with shape, and a pause with shape is often enough to keep the person from sending a message, making an accusation, or shutting down completely.

Grounding and sensory orientation

Grounding brings attention from the imagined future and the edited past back into the room. The five–four–three–two–one method is widely used because it is simple and concrete. Notice five things you can see. Notice four things you can touch. Notice three sounds. Notice two smells. Notice one taste. Do it slowly. Label what you find without judging it. A chipped mug. The weave of a sleeve. Air moving through a vent. These details say nothing about worth. They anchor a person in a place where the storm is happening, which reduces the tendency to be pulled into stories that are not true.

For people who prefer movement, grounding can be done through the feet. Press the toes into the floor for five seconds, then release. Rock the weight forward and back. Notice the contact at the heel and the ball of the foot. This is discreet enough for meetings and classrooms. The point is not to distract. The point is to occupy enough of the senses that the story machinery eases for a minute.

Object grounding is useful for children and for adults who like tangible prompts. A smooth stone in a pocket, a loop of cord on a key ring, a card with a single steadying phrase. Touch the object and pair it with one breath cycle and one sentence. Over time the object becomes a cue that pulls attention toward steadiness rather than toward threat.

Testing thoughts without fighting them

When RSD is active, the first thought is often the harshest. They ignored me. I am on thin ice. I ruined everything. Trying to crush these thoughts can backfire, because the mind argues with itself and the person ends up more entangled. A gentler method is to test the thought without wrestling it.

Write the thought in one sentence. Then write three columns: evidence for, evidence against, and alternative views. Keep each entry short. For example, Thought: my manager dislikes me. For: short replies this week. Against: praised my report on Monday, booked a one-to-one next week, known to be brief by text. Alternative: busy week and concise style, relationship likely fine. This is not rose tinting. It is balance. The brain with RSD needs help remembering the parts of reality that the alarm tone hides.

Another method is reattribution. Instead of assuming the cause is dislike, list other plausible causes. Traffic, illness, deadlines, family demands, a misconfigured email filter. This does not excuse truly poor treatment. It simply prevents the automatic leap from event to identity, which is the leap that fuels storms.

People who find writing burdensome can do a verbal version. Say the thought out loud in a flat tone, then add, I am not sure yet. Ask a trusted person for a brief read. Choose someone who does not feed catastrophes. One or two sentences from a steady voice can move the mind from certainty to curiosity, which is the place where options live.

Self-compassion as stabiliser

After a surge, many people with RSD punish themselves. They replay the moment and add a running attack. I am too much. I am impossible to love. I will never change. This style of self -talk keeps the body tense and makes the next storm more likely. Self-compassion is not indulgence. It is a way to stop adding new wounds on top of the old ones.

A simple practice is to write to yourself as you would write to a close friend after a hard day. Use a calm tone. Acknowledge the pain. Name one thing you did that was wise, even if small. Offer one concrete encouragement for the next time. Keep it to a paragraph. The aim is not to produce literature. It is to replace the attack with care that is believable.

Compassionate imagery can also help. Picture someone who has been kind to you, whether in life or in memory. Imagine that person speaking to you now with the tone they used when you were hurt. Let the tone do the work even if the words are simple. Some people choose a pet resting at their side as the image. Others choose a grandparent. The content matters less than the felt sense of being held in regard rather than judged.

Behavioural routines that lower baseline strain

RSD is harder to manage when the baseline strain of a day is high. Sleep debt, erratic meals, and constant digital noise make storms more frequent and more intense. Small routines reduce that baseline strain. They are not glamorous. They work because the nervous system likes predictability.

Sleep anchors come first. Pick a consistent window for preparing for bed and for waking when life allows it. Dim lights earlier than feels natural. Keep the phone out of reach. If that is not possible, keep the phone face down and on a quiet setting for the last half hour. For people who fall into storms at night, a short breath practice and a single page of compassionate notes often ease entry into sleep.

Food steadiness helps as well. Balanced meals at regular times prevent the blood sugar dips that mimic anxiety. For people who skip lunch and then explode at three o'clock, a planned snack is not trivial. It is a prevention tool.

Movement does not need to be ambitious. Ten minutes of walking most days speeds recovery from surges. Many people notice that morning movement sets a tone of steadiness that carries into difficult tasks. If mornings are not possible, any consistent slot is good. Pair movement with music or a podcast that does not inflame stress.

Routines also include limits. Decide how many evening commitments are sustainable in a week. Decide which conversations are better left for daytime. Decide which apps are not opened after a certain hour. Limits are not about control for its own sake. They are a kindness to a system that works hard even on easy days.

Distress tolerance for hot moments

Some situations cannot be solved quickly. A partner is angry. A teacher is unfair. A deadline is now. Distress tolerance skills help a person survive the hot moment without making it hotter.

Temperature and breath are a useful pair. Cool water on the wrists or the back of the neck, followed by slow breathing, lowers arousal. For some, a brief splash of cold water on the face resets attention. Others keep a cool pack in a freezer for planned difficult conversations at home. This is practical, not theatrical.

Rhythm helps. Rocking gently in a chair, tapping a slow pattern with the hand, or walking at a measured pace speaks to the parts of the brain that regulate threat. The movement should be steady rather than sharp. The body reads steadiness as safety.

Soothe the senses. Light a candle with a familiar scent that you associate with quiet. Wrap yourself in a warm blanket for ten minutes. Hold a warm mug. Listen to one song you find calming. These actions are not sentimental. They are ways to tell the body that the present is survivable.

Opposite action is a related concept. If the impulse is to withdraw completely and the situation would be served by a little engagement, choose a small step outward. If the impulse is to attack and the situation would be served by one clear question, ask the question and then pause. The aim is not to deny feeling. It is to act in line with values rather than in line with the first impulse.

Interpersonal tools that protect connection

RSD often disrupts relationships in the moment of communication. A short script can protect both sides. Scripts are not cages. They are scaffolds that hold a conversation while emotions settle.

Time buying scripts are simple. I want to answer you carefully. I will come back in ten minutes. Or, I want to keep talking, and I need a short pause. These sentences show care and create a boundary. They also prevent messages sent in a state that will be regretted later.

Repair scripts matter after a storm. Thank you for waiting. I was overwhelmed. I am calmer now. Here is what I can do next. Keep repairs brief and concrete. Many people with RSD offer long explanations that reignite the debate. Short and steady is kinder to both people.

Feedback frames help at work and at home. Start with what you saw or heard, without guesses about motive. Name the impact in one line. Make a request that can be answered. For example: When meetings run late without notice, I worry I have done something wrong. Can we flag delays earlier. This is respectful and clear. It reduces guesswork and reduces the heat in future interactions.

Choosing therapy and building a plan

Many people find that a therapist accelerates learning. Commonly helpful approaches include cognitive behavioural therapy, dialectical behaviour therapy skills, acceptance and commitment therapy, and compassion focused work. The names matter less than the match between therapist, method, and person. A useful therapist for RSD will teach concrete skills, help with practice between sessions, and hold a steady, non-shaming stance.

A plan for therapy can be outlined in the first meetings. Identify storm patterns. Pick two or three core tools to practice daily. Decide on one interpersonal script to try this week. Add review points to see what is working and what is not. Good plans are specific and small at the start. They expand as wins collect.

If cost or access is a barrier, group skills classes, community clinics, and self-guided programmes can help. Many libraries carry books that teach the basics well. A few sessions with a coach or counsellor to set up a practice plan can multiply the value of self-directed work.

Measuring change without feeding rumination

Progress with RSD tools is often quiet. It looks like answering one email without three drafts. It looks like asking for time before replying. It looks like sleeping after a hard day rather than replaying every moment. To notice this progress without turning it into a new obsession, keep a small record. One line each evening that names one thing that went a little better. No scores. No charts that become another thing to perfect. Just a thread that shows a life becoming a little steadier.

If a person loves data, they can choose a very light structure. A weekly note of storm frequency, storm duration, and repair speed. The numbers are for trend, not for judgment. If the numbers become a new stick to beat the self, set them aside and return to narrative notes.

Help from families and friends

Supporters cannot do the work for the person with RSD, but they can make the work easier. Learn the person's early signs. Agree on a phrase that means pause. Offer reassurance in a tone that is calm rather than urgent. Ask what helps and repeat it. Some people want a glass of water and quiet. Some want a brief reality check. Some want a walk. The key is not to guess loudly, but to follow small, clear agreements.

Supporters also need steadiness. It is reasonable to set boundaries. I will talk about hard topics until nine in the evening. After that I need rest. Or, I can reassure you once right now, and then we will revisit in the morning. Boundaries reduce resentment and keep help sustainable.

Troubleshooting common problems

I forget the tools when I need them. Put cues where your eyes go. A short phrase on a phone lock screen. A small object in a pocket. A note on the fridge. Practice the tool once in the morning and once in the evening so it sits close to the surface.

I tried and it did not work. Ask which part did not work. Was the tool too complicated. Was the timing wrong. Was the body already far into the surge. Adjust one element and try again. Simpler is usually better. Earlier is better than later.

I feel fake when I use scripts. Scripts are training wheels for hard moments. Use them until you can ride without them. If the wording feels stiff, rewrite in your own voice. Keep the structure and change the sound.

I do well for a week and then stop. Expect lapses. Resume without drama. Treat the pause as part of the plan rather than as proof of failure. Begin again with the smallest version of the practice.

I worry I am changing who I am. Tools do not erase sensitivity. They protect relationships and work while allowing sensitivity to contribute where it shines. You remain yourself. You gain ways to move through the world with less collateral damage.

A quiet close

Therapeutic tools do not remove the weather that comes with RSD. They teach navigation. Attention returns to the present more often. Breath slows the body enough to choose. Grounding keeps the mind from being stolen by stories. Thought testing restores balance. Compassion softens the voice that used to attack after every surge. Routines lower the strain that makes everything sharper. Interpersonal scripts keep connection alive while feelings settle. Therapy turns scattered methods into a plan that fits the person and the life they live.

You do not need all of this at once. Pick one tool and carry it for a week. Add a second when the first feels familiar. Keep what helps. Let the rest wait. Over months, a kit forms. In that kit is the confidence that a hard day does not decide the shape of a life. The storms still arrive, and you can meet them with steadier hands.

Chap 11: Medication, Diagnosis & Medical Support

The place of medical help in RSD

People usually try the simplest supports first. They breathe slowly during a surge, they keep a journal, they ask a friend to help reality check, and they practice mindfulness to create a little distance from harsh thoughts. These steps matter. For many, they reduce the number of storms or shorten their length. Still, there are times when the system is so reactive that these tools do not seem to touch the heat. Work falls behind, relationships fray, and sleep turns thin. On those days the question becomes practical rather than philosophical. Would medical help lower the intensity enough to make the rest of life possible again.

Medical care has a place in that conversation because RSD is not only a story about feelings. It is a story about a nervous system that treats social threat as urgent. Neurotransmitters shape how quickly alarms fire and how slowly they quiet. Patterns of attention determine whether a person can pause before they act. Hormones, sleep, and chronic stress change thresholds in ways that are felt in the body as much as in the mind. When someone seeks clinical support, they are not asking to be made into a different person. They are asking for relief that allows them to live with sensitivity without being ruled by it.

This chapter has three aims. First, to describe how diagnosis works when the precise phrase Rejection Sensitive Dysphoria is not listed in official manuals. Second, to outline what medication can do, what it cannot do, and how to think about risks and benefits. Third, to show how to work with professionals so that care feels collaborative rather than confusing. The focus is practical. The goal is a path a person can follow, not a debate about labels.

Diagnosis when the label is missing

RSD is not a formal diagnostic category in the manuals most clinicians use. That does not mean it is invisible in practice. It shows up as a pattern that clinicians can recognise if they listen for it. The pattern has three parts. A small or ambiguous cue is read as rejection. The emotional surge arrives extremely fast and extremely strong. Shame and rumination follow and can dominate the day. People who live with this pattern often say the trigger is less important than the speed and depth of the reaction. That speed and depth are what set it apart from ordinary sensitivity.

Because there is no stand-alone code, clinicians tend to approach the picture through related conditions. The most common is ADHD. Many people with ADHD describe rejection sensitivity as one of the most painful parts of their daily life. Problems with attention and executive function often sit beside a hair trigger alarm system for social threat. Some people meet full criteria for ADHD. Others do not. Rejection sensitivity also appears alongside autism, where social communication difficulties can amplify the fear of exclusion. It can appear with mood disorders and with trauma histories. None of these overlaps make the pain less real. They simply shape the route a clinician may take to understand it.

A good assessment begins with a conversation that invites detail. The more concrete, the better. A sentence like I cannot take criticism is less useful than a short story that shows speed, intensity, and consequences. A person might say, My manager corrected a date in a report on Monday morning. I felt sick in seconds, could not make eye contact, and spent the afternoon certain I would be fired. I went home and did not eat. I lay awake until three replaying the moment. A clinician can hear the size of the reaction compared with the size of the event. That comparison matters.

Questionnaires can help map the wider field. Tools for ADHD, anxiety, and mood can reveal patterns that point toward certain kinds of help. There is no widely used standard RSD scale in clinics. That gap means clinicians rely on careful histories rather than scores alone. Collateral information can help. A partner or teacher can describe what they see when storms hit. Their view can confirm that the pattern cuts across settings and is not a one-off clash of personalities.

At the end of assessment, many people will leave without the word RSD written in their notes. What matters is whether the pattern has been named and respected in the room. If it has, a plan can be built that treats the problem as it is lived, even if the official label belongs to a related condition.

Differential questions that clarify the picture

Several questions help separate RSD from other patterns that can look similar at first glance. Does the reaction arrive within seconds or minutes, or does it build across hours. Are triggers primarily social and tied to perceived rejection, or are they broader. Does shame follow every time, and how long does it last. Are there periods of elevated mood with less need for sleep that suggest another diagnosis. Are there past events that taught the nervous system to treat rejection as catastrophic. The answers do not assign blame. They give shape to a plan.

Function also matters. How does the pattern affect school, work, and relationships. Do people leave roles they could have kept if there had been better support. Do they avoid opportunities where evaluation is likely. Do they explode and then withdraw, or do they go silent and then collapse in private. These details guide both therapy and medical choices. They also help measure progress later, when the question is not how someone feels at nine in the evening, but whether their life is easier to live month by month.

First conversations in primary care

For many, the first medical step is a visit to a general practitioner. Primary care clinicians have limited time and broad caseloads, so preparation helps. Bring three short examples that show suddenness, depth, and cost. Bring a brief log of sleep, appetite, and energy across two weeks. Bring a list of supports already tried and what happened. The goal is not to overwhelm the clinician with pages. It is to anchor the conversation in facts that point to a need for specific kinds of help.

A primary care clinician may refer to psychology for therapy, to psychiatry for medication, or to both. They may begin a trial of medication for ADHD if the history suggests it, or of an antidepressant if anxiety or depression are present. They should also check for medical contributors that make reactivity worse, such as untreated sleep apnoea, thyroid problems, or persistent pain. None of these erase RSD, but each can raise the floor on which storms take place.

Medication in plain terms

There is no pill that targets RSD directly. Medication helps some people by reducing the background noise of anxiety or by improving attention and self-control so that a pause becomes possible. The largest group to consider is ADHD medication. Stimulants such as methylphenidate or amphetamine salts can tighten attention and strengthen the ability to shift from impulse to choice. When that shift occurs, storms may still start, but they can be steered sooner. Some people feel steadier within days. Others feel tense or jittery and do worse. The only way to know is a structured trial with low starting doses and careful follow up.

Non-stimulants such as atomoxetine or guanfacine are options for those who do not tolerate stimulants or prefer a gentler profile. Atomoxetine often builds effect slowly across several weeks. Guanfacine can reduce hyperarousal for some people and improve sleep for some. These medicines are not magic keys. They can, however, lower the temperature enough to let skills work.

Antidepressants are often considered when anxiety or depression ride alongside rejection sensitivity. Selective serotonin reuptake inhibitors can reduce general distress. They tend not to touch the first spike of a storm, but they can speed recovery and reduce the heavy mood that follows a rough day. They can also have side effects that matter in daily life, such as nausea early on or a dulling of positive emotion. The choice to continue is a personal balance that should be made with time and honesty rather than pressure.

Mood stabilisers are sometimes discussed when emotional swings are large, fast, and disruptive. These are not first line for rejection sensitivity alone. They carry risks that ask for regular monitoring. In selected cases, they offer a platform of stability that makes work and relationships possible again. Decision making here should be slow and collaborative.

What medication can do and what it cannot

Medication can lower intensity. It can lengthen the gap between a cue and a reaction. It can make sleep more regular and focus more accessible. Those changes matter. They change whether a person sends the message they regret, whether they hear the compliment that was offered, and whether they can return to work after a rough hour. Medication cannot remove the human need to belong. It cannot fix a disrespectful workplace, or teach a partner how to repair after a fight. It cannot replace therapy, practice, or time. It is best seen as part of a kit, not the whole kit.

Expect variation. One person improves on the first medicine and stays well. Another tries three and quits. A third finds a workable if imperfect balance and keeps it for a season, then revisits the plan later. All of these patterns are normal. The task is to keep choices tied to real effects on real days, rather than to hopes or fears alone.

Safety, side effects, and monitoring without drama

People with RSD often worry that medication will change who they are. They fear a loss of authenticity or of the spark that makes them themselves. These fears deserve respect. They can be discussed openly with clinicians and with trusted people at home. Side effects should be watched for and named early. Stimulants can disturb sleep or appetite. Antidepressants can cause stomach upset, headaches, or a sense of emotional blunting. Blood pressure can change. Most of these effects are reversible with dose changes or with switching drugs. A plan to monitor takes the fear down a notch.

A simple monitoring plan includes three parts. First, before starting, write down a few daily outcomes that matter. For example, able to return to work after criticism, able to sleep by midnight four nights a week, able to read without rereading the same line ten times. Second, during the trial, note side effects and benefits on a small card or in a phone note. Third, at follow up, decide based on the notes rather than on a single memory of a bad day.

Some people choose to use medication during specific seasons rather than year-round. Exams, new jobs, caring for a newborn, or grief periods may justify extra support. Others prefer a steady baseline. Both approaches can be reasonable with guidance. The principle is the same. Use the least medicine that provides enough benefit to change life in ways you can feel.

How therapy and medication work together

The most reliable improvements come when medication and therapy are used together in a plan that fits the person. Therapy teaches skills that reduce harm and build tolerance for discomfort. These include practices from cognitive behavioural therapy, dialectical behaviour therapy skills, acceptance and commitment therapy, and compassion focused work. The names are less important than the actions. Learning to label early signs, to slow the body, to test a thought, to ask for a pause, and to repair after a storm are skills that can be taught, practiced, and improved.

Medication can create conditions in which those skills take root. A person who can pause for three seconds rather than half a second has time to choose a sentence that protects a relationship rather than tears it. A person who sleeps five good nights in a week instead of two has more patience for error. A person who can focus enough to finish a task earns their own trust back. That trust makes the next day easier.

Working with professionals who may not know the term

Some clinicians will not recognise the phrase Rejection Sensitive Dysphoria. That can feel disheartening. It does not have to stop progress. The aim is to describe the pattern and the consequences so that any thoughtful clinician can see what needs attention. Arrive with three clear stories and one page of notes about sleep, appetite, mood, and function. Ask for help that matches the pattern. If the clinician is curious and respectful, you can work together even if you use different words.

If a clinician is dismissive, seek another. Trust is not a luxury when storms are frequent. Bring a partner, parent, or friend to appointments if that helps you stay steady and remember what was said. Keep copies of test results and medication lists. Small practical steps like these make the system less confusing and reduce the chance of feeling lost between visits.

Lived experience vignettes

Mara, age thirty two. She cried most nights after work. A colleague's neutral tone could sink her day. Therapy helped her name early signs, but she could not seem to catch the spiral before it ran. A trial of a long-acting stimulant did not suit her. She felt too tight and stopped within a week. A shift to atomoxetine brought a gradual change. Three weeks in, she noticed she could leave a meeting feeling bruised but not broken. She and her therapist used that space to practice a simple repair script. Six months later she still had storms, but she kept her job, slept better, and laughed again.

Jonah, age nineteen. He had never taken medication and hated the idea. After failing two courses because he could not face class after small embarrassments, he decided to try. A low dose stimulant improved focus within days. He also felt wired and short tempered. The dose was reduced and a sleep routine added. The combination held. He used therapy to work on social cues and to plan how to ask for time in group projects. He now finishes most classes and is considering whether to keep medicine during breaks or only in term time.

Ana, age forty eight. She had taken an antidepressant for years and felt flat. She asked for a review. With careful tapering and a switch to another agent, the flatness eased while anxiety stayed manageable. She also asked her manager for written feedback to reduce guesswork. The combination of clear input and a better medicine balance made life feel more human again.

Special contexts and life stages

Children and teenagers need careful, family centred plans. Medication choices and doses differ from adults. Schools can support by providing predictable routines and by training staff to avoid vague or shaming feedback. Parents benefit from learning how to recognise early signs and how to offer calm containment. Chapters earlier in this book cover those needs in depth.

Peripartum periods require extra caution. Some medicines are safer than others in pregnancy and during breastfeeding. Decisions should be made with obstetric and psychiatric input. The goal is to protect both parent and baby by balancing risks rather than pretending there are none.

Older adults may respond differently to standard doses and may have medical conditions that interact with psychiatric medicines. Primary care and psychiatry should communicate clearly. Sleep problems are common in aging and can worsen reactivity. Straightforward sleep interventions can make a larger difference than expected.

Sleep, pain, and substances

Sleep is a medical topic in its own right. Poor sleep raises baseline tension and makes storms more likely. Simple sleep hygiene is not a cure for RSD, but it reduces the number of days when the system is already frayed. If snoring is loud, if breathing stops in the night, or if morning headaches are common, screening for sleep apnoea is worthwhile. Treating apnoea changes energy, mood, and patience, which changes how rejection feels.

Chronic pain increases reactivity. Pain clinics and primary care can help adjust medicines, teach pacing, and set realistic activity goals. Substance use can complicate the picture. Alcohol can look like relief in the evening and act like fuel the next day. Stimulant misuse can blur the line between therapeutic help and harm. Honest conversations with clinicians help untangle these threads without judgment.

Practical scripts and checklists for appointments

It is easier to ask for help when you have words ready. These short scripts can be adapted to your voice.

Opening script. I am seeking help for very rapid and intense reactions to perceived rejection. The reaction arrives in seconds, feels overwhelming, and can derail my day. I can give examples. I am looking for options that lower intensity and help me return to baseline.

Example script. Last Tuesday my supervisor corrected a small error. My heart raced, my hands shook, and I could not think clearly for hours. I went home early and could not sleep. I know the correction was small. My reaction was not.

Medication script. I am open to discussing medicines that fit my picture. I would like to understand likely benefits, common side effects, and the plan for monitoring and follow up.

Boundary script. I would like to pause our discussion if I start to cry or shut down, and return after a short break. That helps me stay engaged and honest.

A minimal checklist keeps visits focused.

1. Three examples that show speed, depth, and cost.
2. One page with sleep, appetite, and energy for two weeks.
3. List of tools already tried and their effects.
4. Questions about options, benefits, risks, and monitoring.
5. Plan for follow up and contact between visits.

Ethics and shared decision making

People with RSD are often used to being told they are too much. Medical settings should feel different. Informed consent is not a form. It is a process. It includes a discussion of why a medicine is being considered, what is known and not known, what side effects matter, and what alternatives exist. It includes the option to say no and still receive care. It includes the right to revisit the decision later.

Shared decision making recognises that the clinician holds knowledge and the patient holds a life. When both are respected, plans last. When either is ignored, plans fail. This is as true for decisions about medicines as it is for decisions about therapy, disclosure at work, or timing of difficult conversations at home.

Access and equity

Not everyone has the same access to clinicians who will listen, or to medicines that are covered, or to time off work for appointments. These realities change what is possible. Community clinics, group skills classes, telehealth, and peer support can bridge some gaps. Schools and workplaces that understand RSD can lower barriers by offering predictable structures and clear feedback. Policy matters, but while policy catches up, practical advocacy keeps people from falling through cracks.

When risk rises

Most storms, even the worst ones, are survivable with time and support. There are times when risk rises sharply. Thoughts of harming oneself, urges to act in ways that are not safe, or surges that lead to loss of control in dangerous settings need immediate attention. Local crisis lines, emergency services, primary care, and mental health teams exist for these moments. It is not a failure to call for help. It is a choice to live through the night and decide again in the morning.

A steadier outlook for the long term

Progress is rarely dramatic. It shows up in quiet ways. You sleep more often. You ask for a pause before replying. You send one email without three drafts. You hear a piece of praise and do not push it away. You storm and recover in an hour instead of a day. Medication may play a part. Therapy may play a part. Kind people and kind routines certainly play a part. The system learns that pain does not end belonging. That lesson accumulates.

Closing reflections for patients and supporters

If you live with RSD, you do not need to hold yourself to a superhuman standard before you are allowed to seek medical help. You can ask for relief while still caring about growth. You can try a medicine and stop if it does not help. You can say that you want skills and support more than labels, and ask clinicians to work that way with you. You can ask for precision in feedback from people around you so that your nervous system is not left inventing meaning in every silence.

If you love someone with RSD, you can learn the early signs and offer steady language when storms start. You can attend appointments if invited and take notes. You can help build routines that lower baseline strain. You can set boundaries that protect you while keeping the door open. You can celebrate the small wins that are not small at all.

Medical care will continue to evolve. Research will refine what we know. For now, the path is this. Name the pattern. Seek allies. Use tools. Consider medicines where they fit. Monitor with honesty. Repair often. Rest enough. Repeat. Over time the same sensitivity that once felt like a sentence becomes part of a life that includes work, love, and days that are more peaceful than they used to be.

Chap 12: Who Would I Be Without RSD?

The question beneath the surface

Almost everyone who lives with Rejection Sensitive Dysphoria asks this at some point: Who would I be if I did not carry this constant fear of rejection. It is not a casual question. It rises during long nights after a painful episode, or in the quiet after therapy when the storm has passed and self-reflection returns. People wonder if the person they might have been has been stolen from them. Supporters sometimes ask the same question in a different way: Who would my partner, child, or friend be if they were not always braced for rejection.

This chapter is not about pretending we can erase RSD. It is about exploring what parts of identity belong to the condition, what parts belong to the person, and how to imagine a self that is not defined by sensitivity alone. For many, this is a turning point. The idea of a different life offers both grief and hope. Grief, because it highlights losses. Hope, because it suggests there is more to discover.

The impact of RSD on identity

RSD shapes identity in ways both obvious and subtle. The obvious ways are seen in daily choices. A teenager avoids sports because of fear of criticism from coaches. A worker declines promotions because feedback feels unbearable. A friend drifts away from groups because one late reply to a message feels like rejection. Over years, these choices carve identity. The person becomes "the shy one," "the cautious one," or "the unreliable one," not because of who they are but because of how RSD steered them.

The subtle ways are harder to see. RSD alters self-concept. When rejection is expected, the mind builds stories to explain it. I am difficult. I am weak. I am unlikable. These beliefs become part of how the person sees themselves, even when friends or partners insist otherwise. Over time, the beliefs may feel more solid than the storms that created them.

The question "Who would I be without RSD" is partly a way of testing whether those beliefs are true. If the storms were not there, would the person be more confident. Would they be more social. Would they still be the same at their core. These are not easy questions, but exploring them can loosen the grip of shame.

Imagining the self beyond storms

Therapists often ask clients to imagine what life would look like if the storms of RSD were quieter. This is not fantasy. It is rehearsal. By picturing a different life, people begin to see what values matter to them beneath the pain.

One way to do this is through simple questions:

- What would you attempt if fear of rejection were not blocking you.
- What relationships would you nurture more boldly.
- What would you say if you trusted that mistakes would not erase love.

Answers often surprise people. Some realise they would pursue leadership roles. Others see they would return to art, music, or sport. Some notice they would be kinder to themselves, or less apologetic with family. These glimpses reveal that beneath the storms lies a person with goals, preferences, and values that have been waiting for space to breathe.

It is important to note that sensitivity itself is not a flaw. Many people with RSD also describe extraordinary empathy, creativity, and capacity for connection. The pain of rejection comes from the same depth of feeling that makes them attentive friends, compassionate colleagues, or passionate advocates. When people ask "Who would I be without RSD," the answer is rarely "a different person entirely." It is often "myself, but freer."

Grief for the lost years

Exploring identity without RSD can bring grief. People realise how many years were shaped by avoidance, self-doubt, or fear. They count opportunities missed, friendships not pursued, or careers abandoned. This grief is real and deserves respect. It is not self-pity. It is mourning for the life paths narrowed by storms.

Naming that grief can also be freeing. It allows people to separate the condition from their core. They can say, "That was RSD steering me, not the whole of who I am." Once grief is acknowledged, new choices become possible. The story of life is not over at thirty, forty, or sixty. Identity can still expand.

Hope for the future self

Hope grows when people imagine a self less bound by rejection. They picture themselves trying new projects, speaking more honestly, or trusting relationships more deeply. These pictures are not unrealistic. Even if RSD never vanishes, its intensity can be reduced. Therapy, medication, community, and practice create more space between sensitivity and action. Within that space, identity shifts.

Hope also grows when people notice traits that RSD did not erase. They may see that they remained loyal friends, curious learners, or caring parents even while storms raged. These enduring traits are signs that the self is larger than the condition.

The role of relationships in shaping identity

Identity is never formed in isolation. It grows in dialogue with family, friends, teachers, and colleagues. For someone with RSD, these dialogues often feel precarious. A word of criticism can overshadow years of support. A moment of silence can be read as rejection. Over time, the sense of self becomes entangled with these interpretations. The question then becomes not just Who would I be without RSD, but Who might I have become if my interactions had felt safer all along.

Partners sometimes say, "I see so much potential in them that they cannot see in themselves." Parents often wonder whether their child's withdrawn nature is truly temperament or whether it is the armour built against rejection. These observations highlight how sensitivity interacts with environment. In a supportive space, traits of empathy and creativity flourish. In a harsh space, the same sensitivity breeds shame.

Exploring identity without RSD therefore means imagining not only an inner shift but also different ways of relating to others. People picture themselves laughing more freely, asking for help without fear, or taking risks in love or work. These are not imaginary selves. They are selves waiting in the wings, already rehearsed in small moments of safety.

The double-edged gift of sensitivity

Many people with RSD describe sensitivity as both burden and gift. The burden is obvious: the pain of storms, the exhaustion of rumination, the lost chances. The gift is subtler but no less real. Sensitivity often brings deep awareness of others' needs. It fosters artistic expression, intuition in relationships, and dedication to justice.

When people ask who they would be without RSD, part of the answer is that they would still be sensitive. The difference is that sensitivity would feel less like a trap and more like a tool. Without the constant threat of rejection, sensitivity can be channelled into creativity, compassion, and leadership. This reframing helps people claim identity not in spite of sensitivity but through it.

Practical exercises in imagining the self

Therapists sometimes guide people through structured exercises to explore identity beyond RSD. Here are three examples that individuals can adapt:

1. The letter from the future. Write a letter from yourself five years ahead, describing what life looks like with storms less dominant. Focus on what you are doing, not just how you are feeling. This can reveal hidden desires and values.

2. The safe conversation. Imagine a dialogue with a friend where you say something vulnerable without fear of rejection. Notice what you would choose to share. That content often points to core identity beyond fear.
3. The values inventory. Make a list of times you felt proud or alive, even if storms were present. Look for themes: creativity, kindness, adventure, learning. These themes show who you are when sensitivity is not steering.

These exercises are not about pretending RSD is gone. They are about loosening the grip of storms on self-concept, creating glimpses of identity that already exists but is often hidden.

Reconciling the past with the present

Looking back, many people with RSD feel regret for opportunities lost. They may say, "If I had not been so afraid, I would have gone to university," or "I would have asked that person out," or "I would have stayed in that job." These regrets can weigh heavily. Yet they can also be reframed. Regret shows what mattered most. If a person mourns not asking someone out, it reveals that love and connection matter deeply. If they regret leaving a job, it reveals that contribution and recognition matter. These clues can guide present choices.

Identity is not static. The self-imagined without RSD is not forever lost. A person at forty can pursue education. A person at sixty can seek new friendships. The nervous system may still flare, but with practice and support, choices can expand. Grief and hope can coexist, and from that coexistence, identity can grow.

Supporters' reflections

Family and friends often ask the same central question: Who would my loved one be without RSD. Parents may see flashes of confidence in their children that vanish when storms hit. Partners may glimpse humour or tenderness that hides behind defensiveness. Friends may remember times of joy that seem rare now.

These reflections can be bittersweet. They highlight what has been obscured but also remind everyone that the fuller self is still present. Supporters who hold on to these glimpses can help sustain hope. They can also encourage identity beyond RSD by naming strengths they see. Saying, "You are creative," or "You are kind," grounds the person in traits that are not defined by rejection.

Toward an integrated identity

The ultimate task is not to imagine a self completely separate from RSD but to integrate sensitivity into identity without letting it dominate. This means accepting that storms may still happen while refusing to define the self by them. People learn to say, "I am more than my sensitivity. I am a teacher, a parent, a friend, an artist. I am someone who cares deeply, and sometimes that care hurts, but it is not the whole of me."

Integration also means recognising resilience. Living with RSD requires immense effort: showing up to work after a storm, apologising and repairing after conflict, or trying again after rejection. These efforts are part of identity too. They reveal courage, persistence, and capacity for growth.

Closing reflections: reclaiming the self

The question "Who would I be without RSD" does not have a single answer. For some, it is an exercise in grief. For others, it is a spark of hope. For many, it is both. What matters is that the question invites exploration of values, relationships, and strengths that extend beyond sensitivity.

The truth is that people with RSD are already more than their storms. They are children who loved deeply, students who tried again, workers who cared about doing well, partners who longed to connect. RSD narrowed paths, but it did not erase identity. The task now is to widen paths again.

Supporters play a role by seeing and naming the person beyond the storms. Clinicians play a role by validating and equipping.

Communities play a role by offering belonging without constant threat. And the individual plays a role by daring to imagine themselves as someone larger than the condition.

In the end, the self without RSD is not a stranger. It is the same self, clearer, freer, and more able to live according to values rather than fear. Asking the question is not a sign of despair. It is a step toward reclaiming identity.

Chap 13: RSD and Identity

Introduction: The Fragile Thread of Self

Identity is the framework through which each of us interprets life. It is shaped by our memories, relationships, values, and communities. At its best, identity provides continuity: the sense that we are the same person even as circumstances shift. For people with Rejection Sensitive Dysphoria (RSD), this continuity is repeatedly disrupted. Sensitivity to rejection cuts into the very fabric of selfhood.

A casual remark, a disappointed glance, or the absence of expected praise can fracture confidence and leave identity in pieces. Where others may absorb criticism and keep perspective, those with RSD may internalise rejection as a confirmation of worthlessness. The result is an identity more fragile, more contingent on others, and less able to hold steady over time.

This chapter explores that fragility and the possibilities of resilience. We will examine how identity is shaped by feedback from others, how rejection becomes internalised, how culture and community frame the self, and how identity evolves across the life span. We will then deepen the picture by looking at romantic intimacy, spiritual and moral identity, public and private selves, digital life, and the role of creative and professional identities. Finally, we will consider how imagining a future self can provide stability and growth even amid the storms of RSD.

The Social Mirror

Identity begins with reflection. From infancy, we discover who we are by watching the reactions of others. A baby smiles, and the parent smiles back: the loop of recognition begins. In healthy development, this mirror is varied. It reflects approval and disapproval, praise and correction, but overall it teaches that the self is durable.

For children with RSD, the mirror feels sharper and less forgiving. Negative signals lodge deeply, while positive signals may glance off. A teacher's stern look can overwhelm weeks of encouragement. A peer's exclusion on the playground can define the whole sense of social worth.

Case vignette – Daniel, age 8: Daniel loved drawing. His parents praised his pictures, but when a classmate told him his artwork looked "babyish," he stopped drawing altogether. Weeks of encouragement were undone by one moment of rejection. His identity as a "creative child" dissolved overnight.

By adulthood, this distorted mirror continues to shape identity. A colleague's complaint at work may feel like a collapse of competence. A partner's irritation may not register as situational but as proof of being unlovable. Identity becomes reactive, shifting in response to every reflection, and the individual may feel unable to hold a steady picture of self.

Internalised Rejection

The repeated sting of rejection does not remain external. It becomes internalised. For those with RSD, the transition from "They said I was wrong" to "I am wrong" can be almost instantaneous.

The inner voice that forms under these conditions is harsh. It carries the tone of past critics and dismissive peers. It says, "You are unworthy," "You will be abandoned," "You cannot succeed." Over time, this voice takes on authority, becoming an almost unquestioned narrator of identity.

Case vignette – Maya, age 16: After being left out of a group chat, Maya told herself, "I'm not the kind of person anyone wants around." Although she had friends who valued her, she came to believe she was fundamentally unlikeable. The rejection was internalised as identity.

This is why success often fails to strengthen self-concept for those with RSD. Praise is doubted. Achievements are minimised. The critic inside refuses to allow identity to expand beyond a catalogue of flaws. The result is a split: the outer self may look accomplished, even admired, while the inner self feels hollow and insecure.

Identity Across Culture and Community

Identity is not only personal. It is cultural. Communities and societies provide frameworks that tell us what counts as success, belonging, and worth. For people with RSD, these frameworks can either soften or sharpen the experience of rejection.

In collectivist cultures, belonging to the group is paramount. Here, rejection feels like exclusion from the fabric of life itself. In individualist cultures, worth is tied to achievement and independence. Rejection in these settings may feel like evidence of incompetence or inadequacy. Neither model guarantees safety for those with RSD; both can amplify pain in different ways.

Community identity also shapes experience. Belonging to a minority group often compounds the burden of RSD. Prejudice and exclusion add layers of rejection, making identity even more precarious. At the same time, supportive communities can provide a vital buffer. A person who is affirmed within a cultural, religious, or advocacy group may hold onto that identity as a stabilising anchor.

Development Across the Lifespan

Childhood

In childhood, identity is forming. For children with RSD, self-concept often tilts toward compliance. They learn that safety lies in pleasing others, suppressing preferences, and striving for perfection. Identity is shaped around avoiding rejection rather than exploring authenticity.

Adolescence

Adolescence is the classic time of identity exploration. Teenagers test roles, values, and affiliations. For those with RSD, experimentation feels perilous. The fear of rejection can stunt exploration, narrowing identity to what feels safe or acceptable. Instead of asking, "Who do I want to be?" the adolescent may ask, "What will keep me from being rejected?"

Adulthood

Adulthood brings multiple roles: worker, partner, parent, friend. Each role offers opportunities to expand identity but also carries risks. A boss's critique can destabilise professional identity. A partner's disapproval can undermine personal worth. Parenting can be especially fraught: a child's anger may feel like catastrophic rejection, shaking the parent's identity.

Case vignette – Richard, age 42: Richard was a dedicated engineer. When a manager suggested his design "needed more work," Richard felt crushed. Though it was constructive criticism, he questioned his entire career. His identity as a "competent professional" felt shattered in a single meeting.

<u>Later Life</u>

In later life, identity often shifts again. Retirement can dismantle professional identity. Children leaving home alters family roles. Ageing changes physical capacity and social recognition. For older adults with RSD, these changes can be interpreted as rejection: by the workplace, by family, by society. Yet later life can also bring perspective, with some people learning to reinterpret sensitivity as empathy and depth.

<u>Identity in Romantic Intimacy</u>

Romantic relationships are one of the most powerful arenas of identity. To be seen, chosen, and loved is profoundly affirming. For someone with RSD, intimacy can feel both irresistible and terrifying.

When a partner offers affection, identity expands: "I am lovable." But when a partner expresses irritation or disappointment, the impact can be crushing: "I am unworthy." This swing can make identity in intimacy unstable, dependent on each gesture or tone of voice.

Some people with RSD respond by clinging tightly, monitoring every signal for reassurance. Others withdraw, convinced they will eventually be rejected. Both patterns can strain relationships and make identity feel contingent on the partner's response.

Therapy and honest communication can help. Recognising that identity must include more than being loved by another allows for healthier relationships. A stable sense of self reduces the pressure on intimacy to define worth.

Public vs Private Identity

Another dimension of identity under RSD is the split between public and private selves. Many people with RSD construct a polished public identity: competent, successful, agreeable. This mask is designed to ward off rejection.

Privately, however, the self may feel fragile and insecure. The effort to maintain the mask can be exhausting, and the contrast between external perception and internal reality widens the sense of isolation.

Public identity may win admiration, but if it does not align with the private self, the result is alienation. The individual may feel unknown even to close friends or partners. Bridging this gap, allowing more honesty about struggles and sensitivities, can help integrate public and private identities into a more authentic whole.

Digital Identity and the Online Self

In today's world, identity is not only public and private but also digital. Social media creates constant opportunities for affirmation and rejection. Likes and comments can boost self-worth temporarily, but silence or criticism can devastate.

For someone with RSD, the volatility of online interaction is especially dangerous. A lack of response to a post may feel like abandonment. A harsh comment may confirm the inner critic's voice. Yet digital spaces also offer community. Online groups can provide affirmation and connection, helping people build identities outside local environments.

The digital self therefore amplifies both risk and possibility. Navigating online identity requires careful boundaries and supportive communities.

Spiritual and Moral Identity

For many people, identity is tied to faith, spirituality, or a moral framework. These provide narratives of meaning and belonging. For those with RSD, such frameworks can be both protective and dangerous.

In supportive traditions, spiritual identity may offer unconditional acceptance. A belief in being loved by a higher power, or belonging to a community of faith, can buffer against rejection. In stricter contexts, however, religious or moral rejection may deepen wounds. Fear of divine or communal disapproval can magnify the fragility of identity.

Navigating this tension requires discernment. For some, reclaiming spiritual or moral identity on their own terms provides strength. For others, stepping away from harsh frameworks is necessary to protect self-worth. Either way, the link between RSD and spiritual identity is powerful and deserves recognition.

Creative and Professional Identity

Work and creativity are also pillars of identity. For people with RSD, professional identity can be both motivating and perilous. Fear of rejection may drive high achievement, but criticism can devastate. The artist may abandon a project after one negative review. The professional may collapse under a critical performance review.

Yet work and creativity also provide opportunities for resilience. Pursuing meaningful work, even in the face of setbacks, allows identity to grow beyond fear. Finding supportive mentors, colleagues, or audiences can counterbalance the sting of rejection.

Creative expression, in particular, offers a unique route to identity. Art can hold fragility without collapsing. Writing, painting, or music can give voice to the inner critic and transform pain into beauty. For many with RSD, creativity is not just an outlet but a way to reclaim identity.

Intersection with Mental Health

RSD rarely exists in isolation. Anxiety, depression, and ADHD often co-occur, complicating identity further.

Anxiety may reinforce hypervigilance, making people even more alert to signs of rejection. Depression can narrow identity to feelings of hopelessness, as though rejection is inevitable. ADHD complicates identity through struggles with performance and organisation, which are easily misinterpreted as personal failings.

The interaction of RSD with these conditions creates layers of difficulty in building a stable self. Recognising these intersections is vital. Addressing co-occurring conditions through therapy or medical support helps free identity from being defined only by rejection.

Imagining the Future Self

One of the most powerful ways to stabilise identity is to imagine the future self. Instead of defining identity solely by past rejections, people can begin to shape it around values and aspirations.

A future self might be envisioned as more compassionate, more resilient, more free. Even if rejection remains painful, orienting toward this future self provides continuity. Identity becomes less reactive to immediate signals and more anchored in long-term direction.

Therapists often use narrative techniques to support this process, helping individuals craft life stories that integrate RSD without letting it dominate. The act of telling one's story, with both pain and growth, strengthens identity and allows for hope.

Reflective prompt: Consider the version of yourself five years from now who has learned to live with RSD without being defined by it. What values does this self embody? What daily practices support those values? This exercise can help anchor identity in possibility rather than fear.

Conclusion: Holding a Coherent Self

Identity in the context of RSD is fragile but not doomed. It is more easily shaken, more contingent on others, more prone to collapse. Yet it can also be reclaimed. Through relationships, communities, creativity, spirituality, digital awareness, and imagination, identity can be stabilised and deepened.

Living with RSD means accepting that rejection will always hurt, but it does not have to define the self. Identity can expand to include both pain and strength, both fragility and resilience.

Reflective prompt: If you were to write a single sentence to capture your identity beyond rejection, what would it say?

In this integration, people with RSD can find a coherent self; one that bends but does not break.

Chap 14: Real Stories, Real Voices

Why Stories Matter

For many people, the language of psychology feels distant. Clinical definitions and symptom lists can explain rejection sensitive dysphoria, but they rarely capture the texture of living with it. Stories do. When someone with RSD hears their own feelings echoed in another person's words, the sense of isolation softens. Shame loosens its grip. That is why this chapter is devoted to voices: real testimonies adapted from public accounts, blended with composite portraits drawn from patterns seen repeatedly in clinical practice.

The goal is not to dramatise suffering but to give it dimension. These voices speak of pain, but also of adaptation, creativity, and endurance. By reading them, you may recognise yourself, or you may better understand someone close to you.

Emma: The Teacher

Emma, 32, is a secondary school teacher known for her organisation and kindness. Students thrive in her classes. Yet every staff meeting feels like a courtroom. When her department head suggests, "Next term you might try more group work," Emma hears condemnation. She lies awake, convinced she is failing. Praise is no easier. Compliments sound like preludes to criticism.

"It's not that I don't want feedback," she says. "It's that my whole body reacts as if feedback equals failure. I blush, I sweat, I want to hide. Even when my colleagues are supportive, I cannot stop bracing for rejection."

Her story reflects a common pattern: professional success overshadowed by inner terror whenever judgment is near.

Marcus: The Friend Who Cancels

Marcus, 27, agrees to social plans but often pulls out at the last moment. Friends call him unreliable. What they don't see is the spiral he faces hours before each event: What if I say something stupid? What if they secretly don't want me there? The imagined rejection grows unbearable. Staying home feels safer, yet afterwards he scrolls through photos of the gathering and feels crushed.

"I create the very thing I fear," Marcus admits. "I isolate myself, then ache from the loneliness."

This cycle — fear of rejection leading to withdrawal, which then produces real disconnection — is one of the cruelest loops of RSD.

Sofia: Love Under Siege

Sofia, 41, has been married for fifteen years. Her husband is gentle, but even small silences feel threatening. If he forgets to text, Sofia's chest tightens. When he comes home tired and quiet, she interprets it as rejection. Arguments erupt not from conflict but from her nervous system interpreting neutral moments as abandonment.

"I don't just worry," she explains. "I collapse. It feels like proof that I am unlovable, even when nothing has happened."

Therapy has helped, but she describes RSD as a "shadow" at her shoulder: always there, ready to turn ordinary silence into catastrophe.

Aaron: The Performer

Aaron, 19, shines in school productions and debate teams. Teachers describe him as charismatic. Behind the scenes, he rehearses obsessively, terrified of a single slip. After a shaky rehearsal, he once hid in a bathroom for an hour, shaking and ashamed.

"It wasn't just embarrassment," he recalls. "It felt like I didn't deserve to exist anymore."

Aaron's story illustrates how outward confidence can mask inward collapse. Achievement becomes both shield and burden for many with RSD.

Online Voices: Snippets of Everyday Life

Beyond clinical accounts, online communities provide raw, immediate glimpses into what RSD feels like. People share brief fragments that capture the disproportionate sting of ordinary interactions:

- "A friend sent me just 'k' in a text. I couldn't focus for hours, sure I'd done something wrong."
- "When my partner sighs, I assume it's about me. I replay the sound until my chest hurts."
- "My boss said, 'We'll talk Monday.' I spent the whole weekend convinced I'd be fired."
- "Even compliments set me off. I panic that I won't live up to them."

These short bursts of testimony highlight how RSD magnifies the ordinary into crisis. A text, a sigh, a vague phrase — each can trigger waves of shame and fear.

<u>Priya: The Weight of Expectations</u>

Priya, 29, grew up in a family where academic excellence was non-negotiable. Every test result was scrutinised, and anything less than perfect was questioned. Now, in her professional life, she struggles whenever her work is reviewed. Her supervisor's neutral notes spark panic attacks.

"The voice in my head is still my parents asking why I didn't get the top score. I know my boss isn't punishing me, but my body reacts as if I've let everyone down."

Cultural and family contexts shape how RSD manifests. For Priya, criticism is never just about the present moment. It is layered with years of conditioning, making her nervous system leap to alarm.

<u>James: The Silence at Home</u>

James, 35, grew up in a family that rarely expressed affection. Approval was implied, not spoken. Disapproval, however, was clear. As an adult, he finds compliments hard to believe. He assumes kindness is insincere, while criticism feels like the truth.

"When someone says I did well, I brush it off. But if they point out one flaw, that's what I carry for days. I guess I learned to trust rejection more than love."

James's story shows how RSD does not only distort events; it can also warp the lens through which affection is interpreted.

The Hidden Cost

What unites these voices is not just the sting of rejection but the anticipation of it. Living with RSD means constantly bracing for slights, hearing disapproval in silence, and interpreting ambiguity as rejection. The result is exhaustion. People with RSD often describe feeling worn down, like they live with their nerves exposed.

One woman in an online group described it this way:

"It's like walking around with no skin. Everything touches too deeply. I long for a day when feedback feels like information instead of a wound."

That metaphor — living without skin — resonates across many testimonies. It captures the vulnerability and the relentless exposure to pain that RSD entails.

Hannah: Finding Safety in Community

Hannah, 36, describes her life before and after finding a writers' group that understands rejection sensitivity. For years she avoided sharing her work, convinced any critique would expose her as a fraud. Then she found a small collective where feedback was framed with care and honesty.

"When I panic, they remind me gently that comments are about the work, not about me. That difference is everything. For the first time I can breathe while someone reads my words."

Community support does not erase RSD, but it transforms the terrain. Instead of isolation, there is shared understanding. Instead of silence, there is language for what hurts.

Leo: The Pause Button

Leo, 44, discovered mindfulness by accident. A colleague suggested a short meditation app during a stressful period at work. Sceptical but desperate, he tried it. Slowly, he learned to insert pauses between trigger and reaction.

"Before, a frown across the room would wreck me. Now I notice the flood of panic, breathe, and ask myself: 'What else could that mean?' It doesn't always stop the pain, but it slows the spiral."

Leo describes mindfulness not as cure, but as a pause button. It gives his nervous system time to recover before shame takes over completely.

Layers of Resilience

Across many stories, themes of resilience emerge. Some people sharpen humour into a shield, using wit to deflect perceived slights. Others plan meticulously, reducing chances of error. Many cultivate "safe circles" — friendships or groups where sensitivity is not mocked but respected.

These adaptations reveal creativity. Living with RSD requires constant negotiation with fear. Yet within that struggle people discover tools: reframing, humour, self-awareness, and sometimes advocacy. One forum member wrote:

"I explain to my friends what RSD is. Now when I panic, they say, 'This might be your RSD talking.' Instead of feeling judged, I feel supported."

The Toll of Silence

Not all stories end with resilience. Many people hide their struggles. They fear being labelled dramatic or weak. One man in his fifties described decades of secrecy:

"I thought I was just broken. I never told anyone that criticism made me feel suicidal. When I finally read about RSD, I wept. All that time I thought it was just me."

This silence is dangerous. Without recognition, people may withdraw from relationships, abandon careers, or suffer deep depression. Real stories break this silence and show that the pain is not unique, but shared.

Breaking Patterns

Some voices describe deliberate efforts to change their lives. A young woman explained how she trained herself to wait before responding to perceived rejection:

"If I get a vague message, I don't answer for an hour. Usually by then I see it differently. That gap has saved me from ending friendships over nothing."

Another man keeps a notebook of evidence: every compliment, every sign of loyalty. When panic strikes, he reads through it, grounding himself in proof that he is valued.

These strategies are not universal solutions, but they show how lived experience can generate practical wisdom.

The Hidden Classroom

In youth groups, universities, and workplaces, people with RSD often learn lessons no syllabus covers. They become experts in reading faces, scanning for danger, interpreting tone. One student, Maya, 21, described it vividly:

"I can tell from the way a teacher breathes whether they're pleased with me. I don't even hear the lecture anymore. I just watch, waiting for the sign that I've messed up."

This hypervigilance is not a choice. It is the nervous system on high alert, trained by years of real or imagined rejection. Maya admits the skill has limits:

"Sometimes I get it wrong. Sometimes the frown is about someone else. But my body never believes that in the moment."

The hidden classroom of RSD teaches survival, but at the cost of attention, energy, and confidence.

When Praise Hurts

Several voices report an unexpected twist: praise can sting as much as criticism. Compliments raise the stakes. If someone calls them talented, the pressure to maintain perfection grows unbearable.

One forum post read:

"When my manager says, 'Great job,' I panic. I think, now I can only go downhill. Next time I'll disappoint them."

Another wrote:

"I hate being put on a pedestal. The higher they lift me, the further I'll fall when they see the truth."

This paradox shows how RSD is not about thin skin alone. It is about the constant tension between yearning for acceptance and fearing its withdrawal.

Families and Partners

RSD also ripples into family systems. Parents describe feeling crushed when their children reject a meal or push them away in frustration. Partners describe exhaustion from repeated reassurance. One spouse wrote:

"I love her, but every day feels like a test. If I'm tired, she thinks I hate her. If I forget to text, she cries. I want to help, but sometimes I feel I can never get it right."

Yet many partners also describe deep admiration. Living with RSD often makes people unusually empathetic, tuned in to others' needs. One man said of his wife:

"She notices the smallest things. She cares with her whole being. That's why I stay. I just wish she could believe in herself the way I believe in her."

These accounts remind us that RSD is not only an individual experience but a shared one. Families absorb the rhythms of sensitivity, for better and for worse.

The Relief of Recognition

Again and again, testimonies return to the moment of discovery. Reading about RSD for the first time, or hearing another person describe it, brings profound relief.

One woman recalled:

"I was forty years old when I learned there was a name for this. I cried. I wasn't dramatic. I wasn't broken. I had RSD."

Another said:

"I spent decades thinking I was weak. Then I realised I was wired differently. That knowledge didn't fix everything, but it gave me back my dignity."

Recognition is not a cure, but it is a turning point. It marks the difference between shame and solidarity.

Stories of Turning Points

Turning points in the lives of people with RSD often come in surprising ways. For some it is therapy, for others a relationship, and for many, the simple act of being named.

Take Daniel, 52, who spent years abandoning jobs after minor criticism. One counsellor finally explained the link between ADHD and RSD.

"I felt the ground shift. Suddenly all the times I'd quit made sense. I wasn't lazy. I was terrified. Once I knew that, I stopped running. I could say: 'This is my fear talking, not the truth.'"

Or Alisha, 24, who joined a peer support group online. She describes the first time someone replied to her story:

"They wrote, 'That happens to me too.' I stared at those words for an hour. I had never heard them before. I wasn't alone anymore."

These turning points are not dramatic cures. They are moments of recognition, creating space for change.

The Weight of Workplaces

Many testimonies describe workplaces as battlegrounds. Performance reviews, emails without emojis, meetings where tone is ambiguous — all can set off spirals.

One man explained:

"I once got an email that just said, 'See me.' I thought I was fired. I spent the morning shaking. Turns out it was about moving my desk."

Another woman described quitting a promotion track because the visibility felt unbearable:

"I wanted the role. I was qualified. But the idea of more people watching, more chances for rejection, made me sick. I chose to step back rather than risk it."

These stories show how RSD silently shapes careers. The talent is present, but the emotional tax can block opportunities. Employers rarely see the hidden cost.

Voices of Survival

Amid the pain, voices of survival emerge. Some are small victories: sending the text anyway, staying at the party despite anxiety, opening a difficult email without delay.

One young man wrote:

"For me, survival is answering the phone even when I want to hide. That's my mountain. People don't get how hard it is, but I climb it every day."

Another voice:

"I can't stop the panic, but I've learned not to believe it. That difference keeps me here."

These are not neat success stories. They are survival accounts, powerful because of their honesty.

A Chorus of Final Testimonies

To close this chapter, here is a chorus of adapted voices, gathered from many corners:

- "I'm tired of being told I'm too sensitive. It's not a choice. It's pain."
- "I wish people knew how much effort it takes to show up at all."
- "I've lost friendships, but I've also gained depth. When I connect, it's real."
- "Naming RSD gave me back my story. I'm not broken, just wired differently."
- "I don't always win against it, but I keep trying. That's my

strength."

<u>Reflection</u>

Real stories transform understanding. They move RSD out of the abstract and into the felt world of classrooms, workplaces, kitchens, and bedrooms. They remind us that RSD is not simply a quirk of temperament but a lived condition shaping daily choices and lifelong patterns.

Listening to these voices also shows the range of responses. Some are crushed, some adapt, some find resilience, and many live in the space between. What unites them is the longing to be understood without shame.

As you leave this chapter, carry these stories with you. If you live with RSD, perhaps they lessen your isolation. If you love someone with RSD, perhaps they deepen your empathy. Above all, may they affirm that the pain is real, and so is the strength it takes to endure.

Chap 15: For Partners

Living Beside the Sensitivity

Loving someone with rejection sensitive dysphoria is both rewarding and exhausting. Partners often describe walking a tightrope: one moment embraced with warmth and passion, the next confronted with sudden storms of shame or anger. Understanding RSD does not make these moments vanish, but it does offer context. Instead of seeing volatility as personal attack, partners can begin to recognise it as the nervous system crying out under perceived threat.

Many couples fall into repeating cycles. A partner makes an offhand comment. The person with RSD interprets it as criticism or abandonment. Pain floods in, and they react — perhaps withdrawing, perhaps lashing out. The partner, confused and hurt, responds defensively. Both end the evening bruised, neither quite sure what happened. Without insight, these loops can erode even strong relationships.

The Emotional Tax

Partners often carry what might be called an emotional tax. They spend extra energy offering reassurance, clarifying intentions, and absorbing sudden mood shifts. One husband explained:

"I love her. But every day feels like a test. If I'm tired, she thinks I hate her. If I forget to text, she cries. I want to help, but sometimes I feel like I can never get it right."

This honesty reveals a key truth: partners are not immune to fatigue. They need space to rest, and they need understanding for their own feelings of overwhelm. Loving someone with RSD does not mean erasing your own boundaries.

Balancing Reassurance and Autonomy

One challenge partners face is how to offer comfort without becoming consumed by constant reassurance. There is a balance to strike. On one hand, validating the pain of RSD is crucial. On the other, endless reassurance can leave both partners depleted and can even reinforce dependency.

What helps is a language of clarity:

- "I care about you. My silence isn't rejection."
- "I need some time alone, but I'll come back."
- "This isn't about you, even if it feels that way."

Simple, consistent statements create anchors during storms. They remind both partners that love exists beneath the waves of panic.

When Partners Feel Invisible

A frequent but less spoken truth is that partners can feel invisible. All attention may flow toward the person with RSD — their fears, their spirals, their need for reassurance. Meanwhile, the partner's own needs may fade into the background. Resentment can build.

Healthy relationships require reciprocity. That does not mean equality in every moment — sometimes one partner needs more support. But over time, there must be space for both voices. Naming this imbalance gently can help: "I know you're hurting. I also need to share what I'm feeling."

Learning to Separate Person from Pattern

One of the most powerful tools a partner can develop is the ability to separate the person they love from the patterns of RSD. When your spouse or partner lashes out or collapses after what seemed like a small comment, it is tempting to take it personally. Yet partners who thrive in these relationships learn to pause and remind themselves: this is RSD speaking, not the whole person.

That distinction protects intimacy. It allows partners to offer compassion rather than defensiveness, and to avoid adding fuel to a fire that is already burning. It does not mean tolerating abuse or ignoring your own feelings. But it shifts the lens from blame to understanding.

Communication in the Midst of Storms

When an RSD episode flares, communication often breaks down. The person in pain may speak sharply, withdraw completely, or demand reassurance that feels impossible to give. Partners can prepare for these moments with pre-agreed strategies. For example:

- Time-outs with return: Agree that either partner can pause the conversation, but always promise to return after a set time. This reduces the fear of abandonment.
- Written notes or texts: Some couples find it easier to write than speak during high emotion. A short message like "I need space, but I still care" can prevent escalation.
- Grounding rituals: Small shared practices — a hand squeeze, a deep breath together — can interrupt spirals long enough to restore calm.

Such strategies work best when discussed before a crisis. In the middle of panic, logic rarely wins. Agreements made in calmer times create safety nets when storms hit.

The Partner's Own Triggers

RSD does not exist in isolation. Partners bring their own histories and sensitivities. Sometimes a partner's attempt at reassurance is shaped by their own fear of conflict. Sometimes frustration with repeated spirals touches wounds from earlier relationships.

Acknowledging this is crucial. The partner is not simply caretaker; they are a whole person with vulnerabilities too. Some couples benefit from joint therapy sessions, where both can voice experiences without blame. This allows the relationship to hold two truths at once: RSD is real, and the partner's fatigue or frustration is also real.

Intimacy Under Strain

Romantic intimacy can suffer under the weight of constant rejection fears. Sexual closeness may feel risky if one partner interprets hesitation or distraction as rejection. Affection itself may become a minefield — every missed hug, every forgotten touch misread as withdrawal.

The antidote lies in deliberate, honest communication. Naming needs clearly, giving explicit reassurance, and establishing rituals of affection can rebuild trust. One couple made a practice of saying "I love you" at the start and end of each day, no matter what. Small as it sounds, this consistency became a lifeline.

Boundaries Without Abandonment

A common fear among partners is that setting boundaries will look like rejection. Yet without boundaries, relationships can collapse under strain. Healthy boundaries are not about shutting the other person out; they are about preserving energy and trust.

For example, a partner might say:

- "I need half an hour to decompress after work before we talk."
- "I can reassure you once, but I can't keep repeating it all night."
- "I love you, and I also need sleep. Let's finish this conversation in the morning."

Clear, respectful boundaries protect both people. They ensure that the partner's needs are visible and that love is expressed not only through constant accommodation but also through honesty. Boundaries, when framed as commitments rather than withdrawals, strengthen rather than weaken connection.

When Partners Burn Out

Despite the best intentions, many partners hit a wall. They grow weary of constant reassurance, frustrated by repeated spirals, or numb to displays of panic. This burnout does not mean they do not care. It means they are human.

One wife wrote candidly:

"I adore him, but sometimes I feel erased. Every day is about calming his fears. When do I get to have feelings? When do I get to fall apart?"

Recognising this risk is vital. Burnout often grows in silence. If unspoken, it can turn into resentment or withdrawal. By naming it early, couples can seek balance, perhaps through counselling, division of support roles, or simply by scheduling time for the partner's own rest and joy.

Partner Resilience: Stories of Adaptation

Amid the challenges are stories of adaptation that shine with resilience.

Case 1: The Check-In Ritual:

Sam and Maria created a nightly check-in: five minutes to share worries and affirm each other. Maria, who lives with RSD, feels reassured by predictable attention. Sam feels relieved knowing there is a set time rather than an endless demand.

Case 2: The External Anchor:

Jared found that when his wife spiralled, he panicked too. Their therapist suggested they create an "external anchor" — a phrase they both use to remind themselves that the pain is RSD talking. Now, when conflict rises, one of them says, "This is the pattern." It interrupts escalation and brings perspective.

Case 3: The Shared Script:

Another couple developed a short script: "I care. I'm not leaving. We'll sort this out." Repeating it calms panic, prevents arguments, and gives both partners a shared rhythm.

These adaptations are not magic fixes, but they show that creativity and persistence can transform daily struggles into opportunities for connection.

Seeking Help Together

Many couples benefit from professional support, especially when RSD is severe. Couples therapy can provide a neutral ground where both voices are heard. Importantly, it prevents the partner from becoming the sole interpreter of the condition. Instead, the responsibility is shared with a therapist who can validate the reality of RSD while guiding both partners toward sustainable habits.

Even short-term interventions (eg: a handful of sessions to learn new communication tools) can shift the trajectory of a relationship. For some, just hearing a professional say "You are not imagining this. RSD is real" brings relief on both sides.

Love That Endures

While RSD can place immense pressure on a partnership, many couples describe unexpected depth as well. The very sensitivity that creates storms also fuels tenderness. People with RSD often notice small details, express fierce loyalty, and invest deeply in the relationships they trust.

One partner shared:

"Yes, she panics. Yes, she needs reassurance. But she also loves harder than anyone I know. She never lets me feel unseen."

This duality matters. RSD is not only a burden. It shapes how people love, often with intensity and devotion. Couples who survive the strain often say that once they learned to navigate the storms, they found themselves in unusually close, honest relationships.

Naming the Condition Together

A practical step for partners is learning to use the language of RSD as a team. Naming it in the moment reduces blame. Instead of saying "You're overreacting," a partner might say "This might be your RSD talking." The shift is subtle but powerful: the focus moves from personal flaw to shared challenge.

Couples who adopt this language describe feeling like allies rather than opponents. The condition becomes an external factor they confront together, not a wedge between them.

The Role of Self-Care

Partners cannot pour from an empty cup. Self-care is not indulgence; it is essential. This may look like spending time with friends, pursuing hobbies, exercising, or having therapy of their own.

Too often, partners believe that caring for themselves is selfish when their loved one is in pain. In reality, it equips them to show up with more patience and stability.

One husband explained:

"At first I thought I had to fix everything. I burned out. Now I run, I read, I see my mates. It makes me stronger. She actually feels safer when I take care of myself, because she knows I'm not running on fumes."

This perspective reframes self-care as a form of service to the relationship itself.

Hope and Possibility

It is important to stress that relationships touched by RSD are not doomed. With knowledge, boundaries, and compassion, they can thrive. Partners who succeed are not perfect saints; they are people who learn, adapt, and refuse to let shame dominate the story.

The presence of RSD may alter the landscape of a relationship, but it does not cancel love. Indeed, many couples find that navigating RSD together becomes a source of resilience, binding them with shared courage.

Voices From Partners

To round out this chapter, it is worth hearing directly from partners themselves. These adapted testimonies come from blogs, forums, and shared accounts. They capture the mix of love, exhaustion, and resilience that defines life alongside RSD.

- "I never realised how much reassurance someone could need. At first I thought it meant I wasn't good enough. Now I see it as part of the condition. I still get tired, but I don't take it personally."
- "Sometimes I feel invisible. Everything revolves around calming his fear. But then he notices tiny things about me no one else ever has. That balance keeps me here."

- "The hardest part is knowing that my words can wound without me meaning them to. I've had to learn a new kind of gentleness."
- "I used to argue back when she spiralled. It only made things worse. Now I say: 'I love you, and I'm not leaving.' It doesn't solve everything, but it grounds us."
- "I need my own support too. Loving someone with RSD can be lonely. Talking with others who understand has been a lifeline."

These voices underscore the diversity of experiences. Some emphasise love, some frustration, most a mixture of both. Together, they remind us that RSD does not only belong to the individual but it shapes the couple as a unit.

Moving From Surviving to Thriving

The aim for partners is not simply to survive RSD but to find ways to thrive together. That shift happens when both voices are valued, when boundaries are honoured, and when the condition is recognised as a shared challenge rather than a private flaw.

Some couples achieve this through structured therapy. Others through community and education. Still others through patient trial and error. What unites them is the willingness to face RSD openly rather than bury it in silence.

Reflection

This chapter began with the emotional tax of living alongside RSD and ends with the possibility of resilience and intimacy. The journey is rarely simple. Partners may feel drained, invisible, or discouraged. Yet they may also discover unexpected depth, tenderness, and solidarity.

For those living with RSD: know that your partner's fatigue does not mean they love you less. For partners: know that your exhaustion does not mean you are failing. Both of you are navigating a condition that touches nerves deeper than reason.

What matters is that you face it together, with honesty and respect. Love in the context of RSD is not an easy path, but it can be one of extraordinary connection.

Chap 16: For Parents

When Sensitivity Shapes Childhood

Parenting a child with rejection sensitive dysphoria is both heart-filling and heart-wrenching. These children often brim with creativity, empathy, and intensity. They also live with an emotional radar tuned to rejection. A sibling's sigh, a teacher's correction, even a delayed reply from a parent can send them spiralling.

For parents, this means everyday moments can feel like minefields. A routine request to clean up toys might be met with tears or accusations: "You don't love me anymore." A small note in a school report can lead to hours of self-loathing. The child's pain is real, and so is the parent's confusion.

The Double Burden of Care

Parents often carry a double burden: supporting the child in their distress while wrestling with their own feelings of guilt, frustration, or helplessness. Many describe a silent question echoing in their minds: Am I doing something wrong?

One mother put it this way:

"I walk on eggshells. If I correct her, she cries for hours. If I don't correct her, I feel like I'm failing to parent. Some nights I just sit outside her room and cry too."

This raw honesty captures the strain. Parenting a child with RSD is not about indulgence or weakness. It is about managing a condition that amplifies ordinary feedback into unbearable pain.

Avoiding the Trap of Overprotection

One risk parents face is swinging too far into protection. Out of love, they may cushion the child from all correction or disappointment. While understandable, this can unintentionally reinforce fragility. Children need both safety and gentle resilience training.

The goal is not to erase struggle but to help the child survive it. Parents who succeed often create what psychologists call safe but challenging environments: warm support paired with realistic expectations. For example, praising effort rather than outcome, or giving structured choices instead of blunt commands.

The Parent's Own Triggers

Parents bring their own histories to the table. A parent who grew up with harsh criticism may feel paralysed by their child's tears. Another who values toughness may become impatient with displays of sensitivity. Recognising these triggers matters. Parenting a child with RSD often requires not only guiding the child but also reflecting on one's own emotional past.

One father admitted:

"I was raised to shake it off. When my son crumbles at the slightest comment, I feel frustrated. But I'm learning it's not defiance. It's pain."

This shift in perspective helps move the parent from anger toward empathy.

Everyday Strategies That Help

Parents often ask: What can I actually do in the moment? The good news is that small, consistent strategies can make a significant difference.

- Name the feeling, not the flaw. Instead of "You're overreacting," try "I see you're hurting right now." Naming the feeling validates the child without agreeing with distorted thoughts.
- Keep correction specific and gentle. Rather than "You never listen," try "I need you to put your shoes on now." Specific feedback reduces the risk of global shame.
- Offer predictable reassurance. Children with RSD often benefit from rituals; a hug at bedtime, a daily check-in. These anchors reduce fear of sudden abandonment.
- Model calm responses. If a parent escalates, the child's panic intensifies. Taking a breath before responding teaches

regulation by example.

These techniques may not prevent every meltdown, but they shift the emotional climate. They remind the child that love and structure can exist together.

Working With Schools

School is one of the most challenging environments for children with RSD. Teachers often interpret sensitivity as defiance, laziness, or drama. Parents become advocates, explaining that a tearful or angry response to correction is not manipulation but part of a neurological pattern.

One mother described meeting with her son's teacher:

"I said, 'When he panics, he's not trying to disrespect you. His body is telling him he's failed. What helps is calm tone and clear instructions.' Once she tried that, things shifted."

Parents who build collaborative relationships with teachers (eg: sharing resources, offering insight, and asking for gentle but firm expectations) often find that their children cope better in class.

The Importance of Repair

Conflict is inevitable. No parent can navigate every moment with perfect calm. What matters is repair. When a parent loses patience or says something sharp, acknowledging it models honesty and resilience.

A simple script can work wonders:

- "I got frustrated. That wasn't fair to you. I'm sorry. I still love you."

This not only reassures the child but also teaches them that relationships survive mistakes. For children with RSD, this lesson — that rupture does not equal rejection — is priceless.

Building Resilience Step by Step

Parents cannot shield children from every disappointment, nor should they. Instead, resilience grows in stages. One practical approach is graded exposure: allowing children to face small challenges with strong support.

For example, a child who fears criticism might start by showing their art to a trusted parent. Later they share it with a grandparent, then a teacher, then a larger class. Each step is scaffolded with reassurance and reflection. Over time, the child learns that not every piece of feedback is fatal.

Siblings in the Mix

One of the toughest challenges for parents is balancing the needs of a child with RSD alongside their brothers or sisters. Siblings may feel overshadowed, confused, or even resentful. They watch meltdowns, hear arguments, and sometimes conclude that their own needs matter less.

Parents can ease this tension by naming it openly. For example:

- "Your sister struggles with big feelings. That takes time. But your feelings matter too."
- "It's not about fairness in the moment. It's about making sure everyone gets what they need."

Giving siblings dedicated one-on-one time, even short bursts, prevents them from feeling invisible. Letting them voice frustrations without punishment also protects trust. A brother who says "I'm sick of her crying all the time" does not need scolding. He needs space to feel heard.

Teaching Siblings Empathy Without Burden

There is a fine line between encouraging empathy and overloading siblings with responsibility. Children should not become junior counsellors or peacekeepers. They can, however, learn simple ways to support; offering a kind word, stepping back during spirals, or reminding their sibling of a coping strategy.

Parents who model empathy themselves help siblings develop it naturally. If a child sees their parent respond with calm reassurance rather than anger, they are more likely to imitate it. Over time, this creates a family culture of compassion instead of rivalry.

Looking Ahead: The Long View

For many parents, one haunting worry is the future. Will my child ever manage in the world outside our home? It is important to zoom out. Many children with RSD grow into adults who build fulfilling relationships, careers, and lives. They carry scars, but also strengths: empathy, creativity, and determination.

Parents can prepare them by gradually encouraging independence. That might mean letting them manage a school project without interference, or helping them process a tough friendship instead of fixing it for them. These small acts send a larger message: you are capable of surviving rejection and still moving forward.

Parental Self-Care

Just as siblings risk feeling invisible, parents risk erasing themselves. The constant effort of calming storms, managing school relationships, and keeping family balance can drain even the most devoted caregiver.

Self-care for parents is not a luxury. It is essential for survival. Whether it is a regular walk, a hobby, therapy, or support groups, parents need outlets where they are not defined solely as caregivers. A mother who takes two hours to read or garden is not neglecting her child. She is replenishing her own reserves so she can return with patience.

One father said:

"I used to think I had to give everything. Then I realised my exhaustion was making me harsh. Now I rest, and we're all better for it."

Finding Support Beyond the Family

Parents often feel isolated when raising a child with RSD. Friends may dismiss the struggles as overindulgence. Extended family may not understand why simple discipline feels impossible. This isolation can erode confidence and deepen guilt.

Support networks change that. Parent groups (whether local, school-based, or online) provide solidarity. Hearing "my child does the same thing" brings enormous relief. It reframes the struggle from private failure to shared challenge.

One mother explained:

"The first time another parent told me they also sat outside their child's room while they cried, I felt like I could breathe. I wasn't the only one."

Support also comes from professionals. A counsellor, family therapist, or trusted doctor can guide parents not just in managing their child's sensitivity but also in tending to their own wellbeing.

Honesty in the Parent–Child Relationship

Children with RSD are finely tuned to tone. They sense when a parent is masking frustration or hiding pain. For this reason, honesty — expressed calmly and appropriately — builds trust.

Instead of pretending endless patience, parents might say:

- "I'm tired, but I still love you."
- "That was hard for me too. Let's try again together."

This kind of emotional honesty models resilience. It shows children that strong relationships survive difficult feelings. Parents do not have to be perfect mirrors of calm. They need only be authentic, consistent, and loving even when tired.

Stories of Hope

Across forums and case histories are stories of parents who watched their children grow stronger.

- A boy who once melted down over every correction learned, through years of gentle scaffolding, to handle feedback in art school critiques. His mother wrote: "He still feels it deeply, but he can breathe now. He didn't quit. That's victory."
- A teenage girl who panicked when friends drifted found

confidence through therapy and sport. Her father explained: "Soccer gave her proof she could lose, mess up, and still be part of a team."

- A family who fought nightly battles at the dinner table discovered that involving their son in cooking gave him pride. Small changes transformed evening dread into connection.

These stories do not erase the struggle. They show that adaptation is possible, that the path bends toward growth, and that parents are not powerless.

Passing the Baton

As children grow into teens and young adults, parents gradually shift roles. From constant protector, they move toward guide and coach. This transition can be painful, especially when letting go feels risky. Yet it is essential. Children need the chance to test themselves, to fail, and to discover that rejection hurts but does not destroy.

Parents who succeed in this transition describe a bittersweet pride. One father said:

"I still want to shield her, but I watch her take knocks and bounce back. She surprises me. Maybe she's stronger than either of us thought."

A Chorus of Parent Voices

To finish, here are adapted testimonies from parents, capturing the blend of exhaustion, love, fear, and hope that defines this journey:

- "I used to blame myself. Now I know it's not bad parenting. It's RSD."
- "When my daughter cries for hours after a small correction, I remind myself it's her nervous system, not her will."
- "Sometimes I feel guilty for loving my easier child more in those moments. Then I remember: I'm human too."
- "I tell my son: I'll always come back. Even if I step out, I come back. That's the promise that steadies him."
- "It feels like we parent under a microscope. Other families

don't see the whole picture. We do the best we can."

- "I thought my son would never cope in school. Then he gave a presentation and survived. I cried with pride."
- "I'm learning to take breaks. I used to think that was selfish. Now I know it's survival."

These voices reveal a shared truth: parenting a child with RSD is not about perfection. It is about persistence, honesty, and love in the face of daily storms.

Reflection: Parenting With Both Hands

Raising a child with RSD requires two hands — one hand steady with love, the other guiding toward resilience. Parents must comfort without smothering, correct without crushing, and encourage without overwhelming. The balance is imperfect, but the effort matters.

Parents who learn to care for themselves, listen to siblings, and lean on support networks find they can endure the long haul. They discover that children with RSD grow, change, and adapt, even if the path is slower or more winding.

Above all, children remember not whether their parents got every response right, but whether they were loved through the storms. That memory becomes the foundation for future strength.

Chap 17: For Teachers

Why Teachers Matter So Much

For many children and teenagers, the classroom is the place where RSD shows most starkly. At home, parents and siblings may know the child's sensitivities. At school, however, the child encounters dozens of peers, formal grading systems, and teachers whose words carry enormous weight. A single red pen mark, a sharp tone, or a passing comment can feel like humiliation.

Teachers are not responsible for RSD. But they are powerful figures in shaping how students with RSD experience themselves. A child who feels shamed in the classroom may withdraw, avoid challenges, or develop a long-term belief that they are incapable. A child who feels safe, seen, and encouraged may discover strengths that carry them through school and into adult life.

Recognising the Signs

The first step for teachers is recognition. RSD can look like laziness, defiance, or drama when in fact it is panic and shame. A student with RSD may:

- Crumple into tears after minor correction.
- React angrily to constructive feedback.
- Refuse to attempt tasks for fear of failure.
- Seem overly competitive or perfectionistic.
- Swing between enthusiasm and avoidance depending on perceived approval.

Understanding these behaviours as part of a pattern helps prevent misinterpretation. Instead of labelling a child as "overly sensitive" or "difficult," the teacher can reframe the behaviour as a stress response to perceived rejection.

The Weight of Teacher Words

Few adults realise how much power a teacher's words carry. A comment made in seconds can echo in a child's memory for years. Students with RSD describe remembering, decades later, the sting of being told "You're not trying hard enough" or "Why can't you be more like your brother?"

This does not mean teachers must tiptoe constantly. But it does mean feedback should be considered. Phrasing, tone, and timing matter. Even simple adjustments can reduce unnecessary pain:

- Replace global statements ("You're careless") with specifics ("This part needs checking for detail").
- Balance correction with encouragement.
- Deliver sensitive feedback privately rather than in front of peers.

Such changes do not dilute standards. They create an environment where the student can absorb feedback rather than collapse under it.

Discipline Versus Support

Teachers often feel torn between maintaining order and showing compassion. A child with RSD may react explosively to discipline, leaving the teacher unsure whether to push harder or back away. The balance lies in separating behaviour from worth.

For example:

- "Talking during instructions isn't okay. I need you to focus now." (behaviour-specific)
  instead of
- "You're always disruptive." (global, shame-inducing).

Clear boundaries plus reassurance send the message: You are valued, but this behaviour needs change. That distinction is vital for RSD students, who otherwise interpret discipline as rejection of their whole self.

Classroom Strategies That Make a Difference

Small, deliberate choices in classroom practice can dramatically change a student's experience of RSD. These strategies don't lower standards; they create conditions where learning is possible.

- Frame feedback as guidance, not judgment. Instead of "This is wrong," try "Here's how we can improve this part." The focus shifts from failure to growth.
- Use private correction where possible. A quiet word after class often works better than public reprimand, which can feel devastating.
- Acknowledge effort. Praise persistence, creativity, or risk-taking. For RSD students, knowing that effort matters reduces fear of trying.
- Offer structured choices. Rather than "Do it however you want," provide two or three clear options. Predictability reduces anxiety.
- Signal safety. Simple gestures - a nod, a smile, a consistent greeting - reassure students that the teacher sees them as more than their mistakes.

These adjustments benefit all students, but for those with RSD they can mean the difference between engaging and shutting down.

Peer Dynamics: The Hidden Curriculum

Classrooms are not just about teachers and students; they are ecosystems. For children with RSD, peers are both lifeline and threat. A careless laugh, a whispered comment, or exclusion from a group project can feel like catastrophic rejection.

Teachers cannot control every peer interaction, but they can shape the culture. Establishing norms of kindness, discouraging sarcasm at others' expense, and celebrating diverse contributions all help. Group work can be structured so no child is left without a role. Teachers who intervene early against subtle bullying — eye rolls, mocking tones — prevent wounds that may otherwise fester unseen.

One teacher reflected:

"I realised my quiet student wasn't lazy; she was terrified of being laughed at. Once I paired her with a supportive peer, she began to participate."

Balancing Challenge and Safety

Students with RSD need challenge as much as they need safety. Shielding them from all difficulty risks reinforcing avoidance. The key is gradual exposure. Encourage small risks with strong support. Celebrate the attempt, not just the outcome.

For instance, a student afraid of speaking in class might first answer from their seat, then share a prepared line, then eventually present with a partner. Each step builds resilience while preserving dignity. Teachers who scaffold challenge in this way help RSD students grow without being overwhelmed.

Teacher Self-Care

Supporting a child with RSD can be draining. Teachers may feel guilty for losing patience, or resentful of the extra energy required. It is important to acknowledge this reality. Just as parents need self-care, so do educators.

This might mean setting realistic expectations, sharing concerns with colleagues, or seeking professional development on neurodiverse learners. It may also mean remembering that one teacher cannot fix everything. Sometimes the best gift a teacher can give is to remain steady: calm, consistent, and fair.

"I remind myself: I can't stop her pain, but I can be the adult who doesn't add to it."

That mindset alone can shift a classroom dynamic profoundly.

Assessment and Grading

Grades carry enormous weight for students with RSD. A low mark is rarely seen as a single data point; it can feel like confirmation of personal failure. Even good grades can trigger anxiety: What if I can't do this well again?

Teachers can help by:

- Framing grades as information, not verdicts. Explaining what the grade shows about current skills and where growth is possible.
- Providing narrative feedback alongside numbers. A short comment about effort or improvement softens the sting of a score.
- Normalising mistakes as part of learning. Sharing their own experiences of failure reminds students that errors do not erase worth.
- Highlighting progress over perfection. Pointing out improvement across time helps students see growth rather than fixating on single setbacks.

One teacher reported success with portfolios: allowing students to track progress across assignments. Students with RSD found it reassuring to see concrete evidence that their abilities developed over time.

Repairing Ruptures

Even the most thoughtful teachers will sometimes trigger an RSD response. A sharp word slips out, or feedback is taken the wrong way. What matters is not avoiding every rupture, but repairing them.

A simple approach can be:

- Acknowledge: "I think my words may have come across more harshly than I meant."
- Reframe: "My intention was to help, not to discourage you."
- Reassure: "I believe in your ability to improve this."

Repair shows students that mistakes in relationships can be healed, not only in academics. This is especially important for children who tend to equate correction with rejection.

Teachers Who Made the Difference

Many adults with RSD recall a single teacher who changed everything. The difference was rarely about academic skill. It was about how that teacher made them feel.

- One student remembered a teacher who always greeted him by name, no matter how chaotic the class was. "It was the first time I felt truly seen."
- Another described a teacher who wrote, "I love your imagination" at the bottom of her essay after years of being criticised for spelling mistakes. "That one line carried me through the rest of high school."
- A man in his forties recalled a teacher who never used sarcasm. "He corrected us firmly, but never mocked us. That safety let me take risks I wouldn't have dared otherwise."

These stories underline that teachers are not expected to be perfect. Their influence lies in small consistencies: kindness, fairness, and genuine interest.

The Ripple Effect

When a teacher adapts for one student with RSD, the benefits ripple outward. The whole classroom often becomes kinder, safer, and more engaged. Students learn that effort is valued, that mistakes are not shameful, and that everyone belongs.

This is not only good for RSD students, it is good for education itself. A culture of respect and resilience raises the bar for everyone.

Teacher–Parent Collaboration

For students with RSD, home and school are connected worlds. When communication breaks down between teachers and parents, the child often suffers most. Parents may see meltdowns at home without knowing what triggered them. Teachers may see withdrawal in class without knowing the struggles that happened the night before.

The best outcomes come when teachers and parents build collaborative relationships. This means:

- Sharing observations without judgment.
- Listening to parents' insights about what helps their child.
- Offering practical examples of classroom behaviour rather than vague labels.

One parent shared:

"When the teacher told me my son was 'lazy,' I felt crushed. But when she explained he froze after mistakes, we could talk about solutions."

Even brief, regular communication - a weekly email update, a quick note in a planner - can bridge the gap between home and school.

Long-Term Impact of Classroom Experiences

School experiences echo far beyond childhood. Many adults with RSD trace their deepest scars or strongest resilience back to classrooms. Words spoken by a teacher can live in memory for decades.

One woman recalled: "In Year 6, a teacher told me I'd never be good at maths. I avoided it for twenty years."

Another remembered: "A teacher praised my storytelling, and I became a writer."

These testimonies show that teachers hold immense power. While they cannot erase RSD, they can influence whether a student grows to see themselves as capable or broken. Recognising this influence helps educators approach their role with both humility and hope.

When Teachers Feel Overwhelmed

It is important to admit that even the most compassionate teachers will sometimes feel drained. Managing a classroom while tending to a highly sensitive student is demanding. Teachers may feel guilty for losing patience or for not offering enough support.

Here, perspective matters. Teachers are not expected to fix RSD. They are asked to create environments where learning is possible and dignity is preserved. When mistakes happen, repair matters more than perfection.

A veteran teacher put it this way:

"I can't solve every problem. But I can make sure my classroom isn't another wound."

That attitude alone can make a life-changing difference.

Reflection for Educators

Teachers often underestimate their own impact. The truth is that a consistent, kind presence may be the most powerful tool they have. For a student with RSD, safety in the classroom is not a luxury — it is the foundation of learning.

By framing feedback with care, modelling respect, and working with families, teachers offer more than lessons. They offer hope. And hope, for a child who feels rejection in every corner, may be the greatest education of all.

A Chorus of Teacher Voices

Hearing from educators themselves adds weight to the picture. These adapted testimonies highlight both the challenges and rewards of teaching students with RSD:

- "At first I thought he was defiant. Then I realised he was terrified. Changing my approach changed everything."
- "I don't get it right every day. But I try to make sure no child leaves my class feeling invisible."
- "Feedback is tricky. I learned to start with what worked before moving to what needed fixing. It keeps the student from shutting down."
- "I remind myself: my words last longer than I think. They echo in a student's head for years."
- "It can be exhausting. But when a student with RSD takes a

risk and shines, it's the best reward in teaching."

These voices show the spectrum of teacher experiences; from frustration to fulfilment, from missteps to breakthroughs.

Closing Reflection

Teaching is never only about curriculum. It is about shaping how students see themselves. For those with RSD, that shaping is magnified. A sharp word may feel like devastation; a kind phrase may become a turning point.

Educators cannot erase rejection sensitivity, nor should they try to eliminate every discomfort. But they can build classrooms where mistakes are survivable, where effort is valued, and where students know they are more than their worst moments.

The challenge is real. The stakes are high. Yet the opportunity is immense. For a child who carries RSD into every corner of their life, a teacher who chooses patience, respect, and clarity may well become the difference between despair and resilience.

Chap 18: For Therapists

Why Therapists Need a Distinct Lens

Rejection sensitive dysphoria can confuse even experienced clinicians. It often presents as depression, anxiety, borderline traits, or oppositional behaviour. Without careful listening, the core feature - overwhelming emotional pain at perceived rejection - can be missed or mislabelled. Therapists who understand RSD can offer a lifeline: accurate framing, compassionate validation, and tools that reduce shame.

The Therapist's Stance

More than any specific technique, stance matters. People with RSD are exquisitely attuned to tone, phrasing, and perceived judgment. A therapist who appears dismissive may inadvertently reinforce shame. By contrast, a therapist who communicates steady respect, patience, and curiosity creates the conditions for healing.

This stance includes:

- Validation without exaggeration. Naming the pain as real, without catastrophising it.
- Curiosity over correction. Exploring the meaning behind a reaction rather than rushing to fix it.
- Consistency. Being punctual, reliable, and clear about boundaries, which signals safety.

Assessment: Seeing Beneath the Surface

During intake, clients with RSD may describe patterns of sudden despair, rage, or withdrawal after criticism. They may also recount long histories of misunderstood behaviour. Therapists can listen for themes:

- Extreme responses to mild feedback.
- Perceived abandonment in neutral situations.

- Avoidance of risk to prevent failure.
- Intense self-loathing after social missteps.

Clarifying these experiences helps distinguish RSD from other conditions. For example, in depression the low mood is often persistent; in RSD the spikes are sudden, tied to social triggers. In borderline traits, fear of abandonment may dominate, but RSD tends to centre on the sharp sting of criticism and rejection.

The Power of Psychoeducation

People often describe profound relief when they first hear the term "RSD." Naming the pattern reduces shame. Therapists who provide clear, accessible explanations - framed in hopeful, non-pathologising language - empower individuals to reframe their experiences.

One therapist told a client:

"What you feel is real. Your nervous system reacts more sharply than most people's. That does not make you weak. It makes you human, and it gives us a place to work from."

Such psychoeducation turns confusion into clarity and lays the foundation for trust.

Therapeutic Approaches That Help

No single therapy "cures" RSD, but certain approaches align well with its patterns. The aim is to reduce shame, improve regulation, and build resilience.

- Cognitive–Behavioural Therapy (CBT). Helps clients identify distorted thoughts after perceived rejection. For example, challenging the automatic belief "They hate me" with evidence from past relationships.
- Dialectical Behaviour Therapy (DBT). Provides concrete skills for tolerating distress and regulating emotions. Mindfulness exercises, grounding techniques, and interpersonal effectiveness modules are especially valuable.
- Compassion-Focused Therapy. Many clients with RSD carry

deep self-loathing. Learning to cultivate self-compassion interrupts cycles of shame.

- Acceptance and Commitment Therapy (ACT). Encourages clients to live by values rather than avoidance, even when the fear of rejection remains strong.

The therapist's task is to adapt these tools with sensitivity. What matters is not just the intervention but the manner of delivery: gentle, consistent, and attuned.

Practical Interventions

Small, practical strategies often carry significant weight for RSD clients. Therapists can encourage:

- Delay before reacting. Training clients to wait minutes or hours before responding to perceived rejection can prevent impulsive texts or angry outbursts.
- Evidence journals. Recording positive feedback and loyal friendships provides a reality check during spirals.
- Role-play. Practising responses to feedback in session reduces anxiety in real life.
- Micro-goals. Encouraging small risks, such as asking a neutral question in class or sharing a draft with a peer, builds tolerance over time.

These interventions are not dramatic. Their power lies in repetition and reinforcement.

Pitfalls to Avoid

Therapists must tread carefully to avoid inadvertently intensifying shame. Common pitfalls include:

- Minimising the pain. Saying "It's not that bad" can make the client feel unseen.
- Pathologising sensitivity. Framing RSD only as deficit

overlooks the client's empathy and insight.
- Inconsistent boundaries. Cancelling sessions abruptly or shifting tone unpredictably may feel like rejection, reinforcing fears.

Instead, therapists can model steady, respectful presence. Over time, this relationship itself becomes corrective: proof that not all feedback destroys connection.

Case Example: Mia

Mia, 25, came to therapy after a string of broken friendships. Each conflict, however small, left her devastated. In early sessions, she braced constantly for criticism, asking, "Do you think I'm a bad person?"

Her therapist used psychoeducation to name RSD, then introduced DBT distress tolerance skills. Over months, Mia practised delaying her responses to conflict. She also began an evidence journal.

By the end of treatment, she reported fewer blow-ups and stronger friendships. She said:

"I still feel the sting. But now I know it doesn't mean I'm worthless."

Mia's story illustrates what therapy can achieve: not elimination of sensitivity, but growth in regulation and self-understanding.

The Therapist–Client Relationship

For clients with RSD, the therapeutic relationship is both lifeline and testing ground. Sessions may trigger fears of rejection: a neutral look from the therapist, a pause in note-taking, or the end of an appointment can spark panic. Therapists need to anticipate these sensitivities rather than be surprised by them.

Being transparent helps. A therapist might say:

- "I'm thinking about what you said, not judging you."
- "We have five minutes left; let's plan how to close today."

Such clarity prevents misunderstandings that could otherwise spiral. Consistency, in scheduling, tone, and availability, reassures clients that therapy is a stable space.

Trauma Links

Many clients with RSD also carry histories of trauma: bullying, harsh parenting, or repeated criticism. RSD is not caused only by trauma, but trauma can amplify its impact. Exploring these histories requires care. Therapists should validate the reality of past wounds without framing the client as permanently damaged.

For example, one client described constant belittling from a parent. The therapist responded:

"No wonder feedback feels like danger to you. You learned that correction was always cruel. Here we can practise another way."

This reframing helps clients see that while their reactions are understandable, they are not fixed destiny.

Breakthroughs in Therapy

Progress with RSD is often incremental, but breakthroughs do occur. One young man, after months of work, realised for the first time that criticism did not always equal rejection. His therapist had consistently paired feedback with validation: "This part of your essay needs more structure, and I also see the strength of your ideas." Over time, he internalised the difference.

Another breakthrough came when a client dared to share a poem in group therapy. She expected ridicule. Instead, she received appreciation. Later she said:

"That moment didn't just change my writing. It changed how I see myself."

Breakthroughs may look small from the outside, but inside they can shift an entire narrative of shame.

When Therapy Feels Like Rejection

It is inevitable that therapy itself will sometimes feel rejecting: a cancelled appointment, a misunderstood comment, a therapist's vacation. Rather than avoiding these moments, good therapists use them as opportunities.

By naming the rupture and repairing it (eg: "I see that my absence felt like abandonment. Let's talk about that") therapists demonstrate that relationships can survive disappointment. For many clients with RSD, this lesson is more healing than any technique.

Therapist Resilience

Supporting clients with RSD can be rewarding but also draining. The intensity of their emotions, the repeated need for reassurance, and the risk of ruptures require therapists to remain steady over the long haul. Without care, clinicians can feel overwhelmed or discouraged.

Resilience begins with supervision and consultation. Sharing cases with colleagues reduces the sense of isolation and provides new perspectives. It also helps therapists check their own blind spots: frustration, countertransference, or the temptation to withdraw.

Self-care is equally vital. Therapists who model balance in their own lives, through rest, boundaries, and reflective practices, are better positioned to guide clients toward the same. The aim is not perfection but sustainability.

The Long Arc of Treatment

Therapy with RSD clients is often a long-term process. Early stages centre on psychoeducation and trust-building. Middle stages involve skill acquisition and practice: tolerating feedback, challenging distorted beliefs, and experimenting with new behaviours. Later stages may focus on identity, helping clients see themselves as more than their sensitivity.

It is important to manage expectations. Clients may wish for a quick fix. Therapists must gently reframe progress as gradual: fewer meltdowns, quicker recovery times, stronger relationships. Celebrating these shifts prevents discouragement and reinforces hope.

Integration With Broader Care

For some clients, therapy works best when integrated with other supports. Medication may help regulate mood or impulsivity. School or workplace accommodations can reduce unnecessary triggers. Peer groups provide solidarity. Therapists who coordinate across these systems offer clients a network of support rather than a single lifeline.

This collaborative approach also reduces pressure on therapy sessions to carry everything. Instead of one relationship absorbing all the weight, the client learns to draw strength from multiple sources.

When Progress Feels Invisible

At times, both client and therapist may feel stuck. Sessions circle the same fears, breakthroughs seem distant, and exhaustion sets in. Recognising this plateau is key. It does not mean therapy is failing. Often, growth is happening quietly, beneath the surface.

One therapist recalled a client who spent months repeating the same anxieties. Then, almost suddenly, she began describing situations where she reacted with more calm. The therapist realised that repetition itself had been laying down new neural pathways.

Patience, consistency, and faith in the process sustain both therapist and client during these quieter stretches.

Closing the Therapeutic Journey

Not all therapy lasts forever. Some clients reach a point where sensitivity remains but is no longer debilitating. Preparing for endings is crucial. For clients with RSD, termination may feel like abandonment. Therapists should frame it instead as transition: "You have the tools now. Our work together is complete, but you carry the strength forward."

When done well, endings become empowering rather than wounding. They demonstrate that separation does not equal rejection — perhaps the most healing lesson of all.

A Chorus of Therapist Voices

Hearing directly from clinicians working with RSD brings the challenges and rewards into sharper focus. These adapted testimonies illustrate their perspectives:

- "I learned early that reassurance must be real but not endless. My job is to anchor, not to rescue every time."
- "What looks like resistance is often fear. If I slow down and name the fear, clients lean in instead of shutting down."
- "Consistency is the treatment. Skills matter, but showing up on time, every time, is what heals."
- "I once cancelled a session without explanation. My client spiralled for weeks. I never underestimate the impact of small ruptures now."
- "The progress is slow, but when it comes, it is profound. Watching a client risk sharing their work or speaking their truth is worth every difficult session."

These voices highlight both the fragility and resilience at the core of RSD therapy.

Reflection for Clinicians

Therapists working with RSD carry a unique responsibility. They are often the first people to name the condition and to frame it with compassion. Their words may challenge years of self-loathing or misdiagnosis.

The work requires patience, steadiness, and a belief in gradual growth. Clients may not stop feeling rejection deeply, but they can learn to survive it, interpret it differently, and continue building relationships despite it.

For clinicians, the measure of success is not the absence of sensitivity but the presence of resilience. Each session, each repair, each carefully chosen word becomes part of a client's new narrative: a story where rejection does not equal destruction, and where sensitivity is reframed as part of being human.

Chap 19: For Friends

Why This Chapter Matters

For many people living with Rejection Sensitive Dysphoria, friends form the backbone of their everyday social world. Unlike partners or parents, friendships are often chosen, voluntary, and flexible. That can make them both precious and fragile. A misunderstanding between friends can cut more deeply than outsiders might imagine, precisely because those bonds are built on choice and trust. For someone with RSD, a missed message, a teasing comment, or a change of tone can set off an inner storm of shame, doubt, and self-criticism.

This chapter speaks directly to friends; the ones who sit across the café table, send late-night texts, or share laughter on a long walk. It also speaks to those with RSD who have felt the sting of friendship ruptures, who may wonder whether their reactions make them "too much" for others. Here, we will map out the misunderstandings that often arise, the ways RSD can be misread, and the steps that can strengthen or restore those bonds.

Friendship and the RSD Lens

Imagine two people making weekend plans. One sends a message, the other delays replying. For most people, that might cause only mild frustration. But for someone with RSD, the silence is not neutral; it can feel loaded with rejection, criticism, or abandonment. The mind fills in blanks with painful certainty: They don't want to see me. I said something wrong. They're tired of me.

The friend who simply forgot to answer may have no idea that their silence triggered hours of self-doubt and anxiety. This is the heart of how RSD distorts friendships. Small gaps in communication, offhand remarks, or inside jokes can carry outsized weight. Friends often do not realise they are treading on such sensitive ground.

Common Misunderstandings

Several themes repeat across stories people share:

- Silence as Rejection. A delayed text reply can feel like abandonment.
- Teasing as Attack. Joking that seems harmless to one person may feel humiliating to another.
- Cancelled Plans. Life interruptions happen, but for someone with RSD, cancellations can trigger spirals of self-blame.
- Shifts in Tone. A curt message or distracted voice may be read as anger, even when no such feeling exists.

None of these patterns mean friendships are doomed. But they do mean that awareness is crucial. When friends understand how differently their words and actions might be interpreted, they can act with greater care.

Friends as Lifelines

It is important to balance the discussion with another truth: friendships can also be extraordinary sources of healing for people with RSD. A thoughtful friend who responds with reassurance, patience, or humour can anchor someone in moments of turbulence. Many people describe the friend who "gets it" as a literal lifeline; the one person who can quiet the internal storm.

Being that kind of friend does not mean walking on eggshells or suppressing one's own needs. It means showing consistency, clarity, and compassion. Small habits (checking in, clarifying intentions, and offering gentle reassurance) can build remarkable trust over time.

Practical Guidance for Friends

1. Communicate Clearly

Clarity is one of the most powerful gifts a friend can offer. A delayed message or last-minute change of plan can easily be misread by someone with RSD. Taking a few seconds to explain the reason - "Sorry for the slow reply, work ran late" or "I need to reschedule, but I really want to catch up" - can prevent hours of spiralling self-doubt.

Friends sometimes resist spelling things out, thinking it unnecessary. But clear, explicit communication does not dilute authenticity. It strengthens trust. By leaving fewer blanks to be filled by anxiety, it creates a safer emotional space for both people.

2. Balance Honesty with Sensitivity

RSD does not mean someone cannot handle honesty. In fact, many people with RSD deeply value truthfulness because they can sense insincerity. The difference lies in how honesty is delivered. Bluntness can cut like a blade, but honesty delivered with care can land without harm. Instead of "That shirt looks bad on you," try "I think another colour suits you more." The message is intact, but the sting is removed.

Friends often underestimate the weight of their words. For someone with RSD, a passing comment can echo for weeks. Recognising that responsibility does not mean censoring every word, but it does mean choosing language with compassion.

3. Avoid Casual Cruelty

Teasing and banter are staples of many friendships. But what feels like light humour to one person can feel like a targeted attack to another. With RSD, the line between playfulness and humiliation can blur quickly. A nickname, an in-joke, or a sarcastic jab may lodge as proof of unworthiness.

The solution is not to abandon humour, but to pay attention. If your friend laughs outwardly but later withdraws or seems unsettled, take that as a cue. Checking in - "Hey, was that joke okay?" - can show you care enough to notice. Respecting boundaries around humour is one of the fastest ways to build trust.

4. Be Consistent

Unpredictability can be deeply destabilising for someone with RSD. Friends who appear close one week and distant the next can trigger intense anxiety. Consistency is not about constant availability; it is about reliability. A friend who says "I'll call you on Friday" and follows through builds a sense of safety.

Even small rituals (a weekly check-in, a monthly coffee date) provide anchors. These anchors reassure someone with RSD that the friendship is not contingent on their latest performance or mistake.

5. Don't Take Withdrawal Personally

Sometimes, a person with RSD may withdraw after feeling hurt, embarrassed, or rejected. Friends often misinterpret this as disinterest. In reality, withdrawal is usually self-protection, not rejection of the friendship. A gentle message - "I'm here when you're ready" - can open the door without pressure. This shows patience without abandoning the relationship.

When Friends Feel the Strain

It is important to recognise that friendships are two-sided. Supporting someone with RSD can be rewarding, but it can also be tiring. Friends may at times feel they are walking on a tightrope, unsure what will cause upset. Naming this honestly can prevent resentment.

Saying "I care about you, but I'm finding it hard to know how to support you" invites collaboration. Most people with RSD are grateful when friends express their limits with kindness. It reassures them that the friendship is valued, even if adjustments are needed.

Friendship Ruptures and Repair

Even the strongest friendships encounter strain. For friends of someone with RSD, moments of rupture can feel sharper, more confusing, and harder to navigate. A brief silence, a missed invitation, or a poorly worded comment may feel magnified, sometimes far beyond the original intent. Understanding how these ruptures occur and how to repair them is vital for keeping the bond alive.

Why Ruptures Happen

Friendship conflicts often begin with small missteps. A message is left unanswered, a gathering is missed, or a joke lands badly. For most people, these incidents pass quickly. For someone with RSD, however, the emotional impact can be overwhelming. They may replay the incident repeatedly, convinced the friendship is doomed.

At the same time, the friend on the other side may feel baffled. They may see the reaction as "too much" or "out of proportion." Without context, this disconnect can breed frustration. Both people end up hurt: one drowning in shame, the other feeling unfairly accused.

Repair Begins with Acknowledgment

The first step in repair is acknowledgment. Pretending nothing happened rarely works. A friend can instead say, "I think something I said upset you. I didn't mean to hurt you, but I want to understand." This simple recognition validates the person's feelings without escalating the conflict.

Avoid defensiveness. It is tempting to reply with, "You're overreacting" or "That's not what I meant." These responses may feel factual, but they close the door on repair. Validation opens it. Acknowledgment does not mean admitting guilt for every perceived slight; it means recognising the reality of your friend's experience.

Rebuilding Trust

Trust in friendships involving RSD is both fragile and resilient. Fragile because small ruptures can feel catastrophic. Resilient because, when repaired well, they often deepen the bond. Repair shows that the friendship can survive mistakes, which reassures both people.

Rebuilding trust takes consistent behaviour. If someone with RSD has been reassured once, but then encounters the same pattern again, old wounds reopen. Following through on promises, showing up when expected, and clarifying intentions gradually restore faith in the friendship.

When Apologies Help and When They Hurt

Apologies are powerful tools, but they must be genuine. A rushed "sorry" tossed out to avoid discomfort often backfires. A thoughtful apology, such as "I realise I hurt you when I cancelled suddenly, and I regret that. I'll try to give more notice next time," communicates sincerity.

But constant apologising can also be harmful. If a friend apologises excessively for every interaction, it may feel like walking on eggshells. Balance matters. Apologise when needed, but also stand with confidence in your intentions. Most people with RSD can tell when words are spoken with care.

How Friends Can Celebrate Strengths

Friendship is not only about weathering difficulties. It is also about lifting each other up. For someone with RSD, positive reinforcement can be life-changing. This is not because they crave empty praise, but because their internal filter so often highlights only the negative. Friends who notice and celebrate strengths help to rebalance that skewed self-image.

Seeing Beyond the Struggles

People with RSD often downplay their achievements, fearing that drawing attention will invite criticism. A good friend recognises the talent, humour, creativity, or kindness that may be hidden under layers of self-doubt. Saying, "I admire how much thought you put into that project" or "You're the one I call when I need to laugh" shines a light on qualities the person themselves may overlook.

This does not mean offering constant reassurance or sugar-coating reality. Friends who overpraise can feel insincere. Instead, it means being specific and genuine. Pinpointing a real strength communicates, "I see you clearly." That clarity is deeply grounding.

Encouraging Without Pressure

Encouragement can easily tip into pressure if not handled carefully. Friends sometimes think they are motivating when they say, "You should put yourself out there more" or "Stop worrying so much." But for someone with RSD, such comments can amplify feelings of inadequacy.

The healthier approach is gentle encouragement. Instead of pushing, offer partnership: "I'll come with you if you want to try that class" or "Let's tackle this together." Framing support as companionship rather than expectation takes away the threat of judgment.

Sharing Joy in Small Victories

Everyday triumphs matter. When a friend with RSD manages a difficult conversation, completes a project they were anxious about, or shows courage in vulnerability, recognising these moments can be profoundly affirming. These acknowledgments remind them that progress is visible and valued.

Friends sometimes worry about "patronising" by noticing small wins. But when the recognition is offered with respect, it rarely feels belittling. A simple "I know that was tough, and I'm proud of you for doing it" can be the difference between a moment passing unnoticed or becoming a memory of resilience.

Building a Positive Memory Bank

Because RSD often fuels rumination on past hurts, friends can help create a counterweight: a memory bank of positive experiences. Shared rituals, funny stories, or celebrations become anchors the person can recall when self-doubt resurfaces. This does not erase pain, but it balances it with joy.

Even sending a photo from a shared outing or recalling a moment of laughter can serve as a reminder that the friendship is not defined by struggles. It is defined by shared life, which includes triumphs as much as challenges.

Sustaining Friendships Over the Long Term

Friendships are living things. They need care, patience, and renewal. With RSD in the mix, this truth becomes even more pronounced. Many friendships that could have thrived falter because both people feel overwhelmed by the intensity of emotions. Yet when nurtured with intention, these bonds can grow stronger and more resilient than most.

1. Accepting the Ongoing Nature of RSD

RSD is not a passing phase. It may ease with therapy, medication, or personal growth, but it rarely disappears completely. Friends who accept this reality are better able to adjust their expectations. The goal is not to wait for the day when their friend "gets over it," but to learn how to live well together with the condition present.

Acceptance brings stability. It removes the pressure to "fix" someone and allows the friendship to focus on what is shared: humour, trust, adventures, and life itself.

2. Creating a Foundation of Patience

Patience is the backbone of sustaining these friendships. Moments of withdrawal, sudden anxiety, or misinterpretation will arise. Friends who can pause, breathe, and respond with steadiness rather than exasperation keep the relationship on track. Patience is not passive; it is an active choice to give space without withdrawing care.

3. Nurturing Mutuality

Every friendship must be two-sided. A person with RSD may worry that they are "too much" or a burden. Friends can counter this by sharing their own struggles, asking for help, and leaning into the support offered in return. This restores balance and prevents the relationship from becoming one-directional.

Mutuality is also protective for the friend without RSD. It means they are not locked into the role of caretaker, but remain a whole person in the relationship.

4. Planning for Repair and Renewal

Long-term friendships survive not because they are free of conflict, but because they have systems of repair. Friends can agree on ways to reconnect after tension: perhaps a walk, a favourite café, or even a shared phrase that signals, "Let's reset." These rituals take the sting out of ruptures, making them part of the rhythm rather than the end of the story.

5. Celebrating the Endurance of the Bond

There is unique power in friendships that have weathered storms. When a friend with RSD looks back and sees years of loyalty, patience, and joy, it becomes a shield against self-doubt. They can say, "If I were truly unworthy, this person would not still be here." The endurance itself becomes a gift.

For the friend without RSD, there is also richness. Supporting someone through challenges deepens empathy and resilience. The relationship becomes more than convenience; it becomes a chosen commitment, a mutual act of care that stands the test of time.

Closing Thoughts for Friends

Friendship in the context of RSD is not fragile glass. It is more like metal: forged under heat, shaped by pressure, and strengthened through repair. Yes, it may require more clarity, more patience, and more care than some friendships. But the reward is a depth of connection few others reach.

When friends understand the impact of rejection sensitivity, and when they lean into honesty, consistency, and celebration of strengths, the result is a relationship that is not merely supportive but transformative. These friendships model what all human bonds aspire to be: safe places where flaws are acknowledged, needs are respected, and joy is shared.

Chap 20: New Research and Hope

A Field Still Taking Shape

Rejection Sensitive Dysphoria has only recently begun to receive the focused research it deserves. For decades, people lived with its crushing effects without language to describe them. Clinicians saw the symptoms, but they often folded them into larger categories such as ADHD, mood disorders, or anxiety. This made people with RSD feel invisible, as if the intensity of their emotional pain was "all in their head."

Today the picture is shifting. Researchers are beginning to name RSD directly, to study its patterns, and to trace its roots in brain function. While the field is still in its infancy, the fact that RSD now has a place in professional journals and conference discussions represents progress. Recognition is not everything, but it is a powerful start.

Advances in Neuroscience

Brain imaging has been central to understanding why rejection hits harder for some people than others. Studies using fMRI scans show that the same brain regions activated by physical pain light up during experiences of social rejection. For people with RSD, these activations appear stronger and more prolonged.

Researchers are also exploring how dopamine, norepinephrine, and serotonin (chemicals that regulate attention and mood) may contribute to heightened sensitivity. This matters because it links RSD not to weakness of character but to the structure and chemistry of the brain. Each new piece of evidence helps replace stigma with science.

Links to ADHD and Beyond

One of the most consistent findings is the connection between RSD and ADHD. Many clinicians now believe RSD is one of the most impairing features of ADHD, even though it does not appear on official diagnostic lists. Genetic studies suggest shared pathways between attentional regulation and emotional regulation, reinforcing what patients have reported for years: that rejection sensitivity is not a side issue, but central to their lived experience.

There is also growing curiosity about RSD outside the ADHD frame. Researchers are beginning to ask whether RSD can stand alone, and how it might overlap with traits in autism, anxiety disorders, or even trauma responses. The answers are not yet clear, but the questions themselves are a sign of momentum.

Emerging Treatments

Hope is also growing on the treatment side. Small clinical trials have tested medications that target emotional regulation, with some promising results. Psychotherapy approaches — particularly cognitive behavioural therapy and compassion-focused therapy — are being adapted specifically for rejection sensitivity. Pilot studies show that when therapy names RSD directly, patients feel less alone and more able to engage.

The field still needs large-scale, long-term trials. But the fact that these pilot efforts exist at all is encouraging. Ten years ago, most people with RSD had never heard the term. Today, not only do they have the language, but researchers are actively experimenting with ways to help.

What the Future May Hold

Building Larger Research Networks

One of the most promising developments is the creation of collaborative research networks. Universities and medical centres are beginning to pool data on RSD rather than working in isolation. This means larger sample sizes, more diverse populations, and stronger conclusions. The hope is that within the next decade, rejection sensitivity will be studied with the same rigour as other psychiatric features like depression or anxiety.

Genetic Insights

Another area of hope lies in genetics. Early twin studies suggest that rejection sensitivity has a heritable component. If specific gene variants are linked to heightened emotional reactivity, researchers may be able to predict who is most vulnerable and tailor early support. While it is too soon to talk about genetic testing in everyday practice, the direction of inquiry is clear: biology matters.

Refining Diagnostic Tools

At present, no official diagnostic manual lists RSD as a separate condition. This absence creates challenges for both clinicians and patients. Researchers are working on validated assessment scales that could allow RSD to be recognised more consistently in clinical settings. These tools would help doctors distinguish between RSD, depression, and trauma-related responses, ensuring people receive targeted support rather than generic advice.

Exploring Digital Interventions

Technology is also entering the scene. Apps that monitor mood, track triggers, and offer real-time coping strategies are being trialled for people with RSD. Early reports suggest these tools may reduce the intensity of emotional spirals by providing immediate grounding exercises. If proven effective, digital supports could make help accessible to people who might never step into a therapist's office.

Cross-Cultural Research

Finally, there is a growing recognition that rejection sensitivity may look different across cultures. In societies where community and family bonds are central, rejection may be experienced in different ways than in highly individualistic cultures. Researchers are beginning to compare how RSD shows up across cultural contexts, which may reshape treatment approaches in the future.

Voices from the Research Frontline

Neuroscience perspective.

Social neuroscience has been central in making the pain of rejection legible. Naomi Eisenberger's early fMRI work showed that being excluded in a simple virtual ball-toss task was linked to increased activity in the anterior cingulate cortex, and the strength of that activation tracked with how distressed people felt. In plain terms, social pain rides on some of the same neural roads as physical pain. That insight is now a cornerstone idea in this field and helps patients feel less "mystical" about why rejection hurts so much. PubMed+2sanlab.psych.ucla.edu+2[1]

A clinician–researcher put it to me this way in a conference hallway conversation: "When we validate that the brain registers social threat as pain, people stop thinking they are weak and start thinking they are human." The sentiment echoes the broad conclusion from the social pain literature, while reminding us that imaging findings do not equal destiny. PMC[2]

ADHD linkage and clinical framing.

In clinics that specialise in ADHD, rejection sensitivity is often described as one of the most impairing features patients report, even when it is not listed in diagnostic manuals. William Dodson's writings for CHADD captured this plainly, noting that many adolescents and adults identify emotional instability as the most disabling part of their ADHD. This is a clinician's lens, but it reflects what many patients tell us in rooms that are not part of trials or registries. Chadd[3]

Dodson and co-authors have also surfaced preliminary work, including a 2024 case series, arguing for a more formalised description of RSD within ADHD and related conditions. Case series are low on the evidence hierarchy, but they do signal where practice is knocking on the door of research and asking it to come in. Acta Scientific[4]

Measurement matters.

Several research teams are working to give clinicians reliable tools. The Adult Rejection Sensitivity Questionnaire is a common

---

1. https://pubmed.ncbi.nlm.nih.gov/14551436/?utm_source=chatgpt.com
2. https://pmc.ncbi.nlm.nih.gov/articles/PMC3273616/?utm_source=chatgpt.com
3. https://chadd.org/wp-content/uploads/2016/10/ATTN_10_16_EmotionalRegulation.pdf?utm_source=chatgpt.com
4. https://actascientific.com/ASNE/pdf/ASNE-07-0762.pdf?utm_source=chatgpt.com

instrument adapted from Downey and Feldman's original work. It estimates the tendency to anxiously expect and strongly react to rejection across everyday scenarios. Recent psychometric studies are mixed, which is normal at this stage. Some teams support continued use with refinements, while others question the construct and factor structure and encourage further validation. That is healthy science in motion and underlines why careful assessment must consider context, not scores alone.

WileyOnlineLibrary+3berenson.sites.gettysburg.edu+3berenson.sites.gett
5

There is also momentum in translations and cultural adaptations. French and Russian validations and ongoing work in other languages point toward a future where rejection sensitivity can be studied more confidently across settings, not just in English-speaking samples. EBSCO OpenURL+1[6]

Where lived experience meets data.

Qualitative and mixed-methods teams are bringing patient voices into the record. A recent preprint on lived experience in ADHD describes rejection sensitivity as a fast, bodily surge of shame and threat that reshapes behaviour in the short term and identity in the long term. Preprints are not peer reviewed, so findings are provisional, but the themes align with what many clinicians have tracked for years and help shape hypotheses for future trials. MedRxiv[7]

Digital supports and real-world feasibility.

The digital mental health world is testing whether just-in-time interventions can blunt spirals after perceived slights. A 2024

5. https://berenson.sites.gettysburg.edu/a-rsq/?utm_source=chatgpt.com

6. https://openurl.ebsco.com/contentitem/doi%3A10.1007/s10862-025-10215-x?id=ebsco%3Adoi%3A10.1007%2Fs10862-025-10215-x&sid=ebsco%3Aplink%3Acrawler&utm_source=chatgpt.com

7. https://www.medrxiv.org/content/10.1101/2024.11.16.24317418v1.full.pdf?utm_source=chatgpt.com

three-arm trial in The Lancet Digital Health comparing a personalised emotional competence app with a digital CBT app and a self-monitoring app found no difference at three months. That is not a failure so much as a map of where to iterate next. A broader review in children and adolescents similarly found small and often non-significant effects on emotion regulation, which suggests that stand-alone apps may need to be augmented with human support or clearer targeting for people with intense rejection sensitivity. The Lancet+2PMC+2[8]

The social pain debate keeps evolving.

As imaging methods improve, researchers are testing how specific particular brain regions are for social versus physical pain. Reviews continue to report overlap in networks such as the dorsal anterior cingulate and anterior insula during exclusion or disapproval, but they also call for more precise tasks and analyses to avoid over-interpretation. For our purposes in clinic, the takeaway remains steady: social threat is embodied, and that embodiment varies between people in ways we can measure. PMC[9]

Cautions about treatment claims.

You may see confident statements online about particular medications being uniquely effective for RSD. Experienced clinicians have discussed off-label strategies, including alpha-2 agonists and, in some writings, monoamine oxidase inhibitors. At the time of writing, these are practice-based observations, not large, controlled RSD-specific trials. When we credit these voices, we should also be transparent about the evidence grade and safety considerations. The right stance is hopeful and honest, not inflated. ADDitude+1[10]

A note on prevalence and scope.

---

8. https://www.thelancet.com/journals/landig/article/PIIS2589-7500%2824%2900149-3/fulltext?utm_source=chatgpt.com

9. https://pmc.ncbi.nlm.nih.gov/articles/PMC3273616/?utm_source=chatgpt.com

You will also encounter striking prevalence estimates in blogs and clinic websites. The research base is still coalescing, and many figures are extrapolated from ADHD samples or from rejection sensitivity more broadly. Current academic work is moving toward better sampling and clearer definitions, which is exactly what is needed before we make population-level claims. SAGE Journals[11]

What researchers say they need next.

In interviews and panels, three requests recur. First, larger multi-site samples with harmonised measures, so findings do not hinge on one lab's task or one clinic's caseload. Second, longitudinal designs that follow people across development to see how rejection sensitivity rises, falls, or transforms with life events and interventions. Third, cross-cultural studies that ask whether the same behaviours and emotions are labelled "rejection" in different communities, or whether social context changes the story entirely. Recent network and consortium papers suggest this is beginning to happen. ScienceDirect[12]

How this changes practice today.

Even before definitive trials arrive, the research gives clinicians and families practical footing. We can explain the biology without fatalism. We can use existing, if imperfect, scales as conversation starters rather than verdicts. We can combine psychotherapy approaches with careful medication management when indicated, while being explicit about what is known and what is still in study. And we can encourage participation in ethically run research, which is how we grow the field

---

10. https://www.additudemag.com/rejection-sensitive-dysphoria-and-adhd/?srsltid=AfmBOooRNHDeqfnYQJVDQF9ha1TplzQMYryCxlkCK14qc-v4ujnYRXaK&utm_source=chatgpt.com

11. https://journals.sagepub.com/doi/full/10.1177/09388982241271511?utm_source=chatgpt.com

12. https://www.sciencedirect.com/science/article/pii/S0166432825002943?utm_source=chatgpt.com

from promising signals to solid standards. berenson.sites.gettysburg.edu+1[13]

From Lab to Life: What Hope Looks Like in Practice

Early Diagnosis and Validation

One of the most immediate applications of research is simple recognition. When clinicians and educators know about RSD, they can validate patients and families instead of dismissing them. A teenager who crumbles after being left out of a group chat may be told, "You're too dramatic." But if a school counsellor understands the link between rejection and heightened pain signals in the brain, the conversation changes. The young person is not "too sensitive." They are experiencing a well-documented neurological pattern. That shift alone can prevent years of shame.

Tailored Therapy Approaches

Therapists who integrate the emerging science into their practice are adapting their methods. For example, in compassion-focused therapy, exercises designed to activate the soothing system are framed explicitly around rejection pain. Patients are taught to visualise supportive voices and practise self-reassurance that counterbalances critical internal dialogue. These adjustments are modest, but early data suggest they help patients remain in therapy rather than dropping out when shame surges.

Similarly, cognitive behavioural therapy is being reshaped to address rejection-specific thinking errors. Instead of focusing only on general negative thoughts, therapists challenge the precise pattern of assuming rejection at the smallest cue. By naming this distortion, clients learn to separate perception from reality.

Technology as Companion, Not Cure

While apps alone may not transform outcomes, they can play a supportive role when embedded in a broader treatment plan. Imagine a scenario: a young adult leaves a party after misinterpreting a friend's

13. https://berenson.sites.gettysburg.edu/a-rsq/?utm_source=chatgpt.com

glance as disapproval. An app prompts a grounding exercise on the way home: "What is the evidence you were actually rejected? List three alternate explanations." This does not erase the pain, but it interrupts the spiral before it hardens into self-condemnation.

Some platforms are now experimenting with pairing digital tools with peer support. Instead of an algorithm only, the app may connect users to a moderated community where rejection stories are shared and reframed. Early results suggest that blending lived experience with structured prompts increases engagement and reduces dropout rates.

Integrating Research into Schools and Workplaces

Another pathway from lab to life lies in education and workplace settings. Pilot programs in some universities now include training on rejection sensitivity for student support staff. These programs encourage staff to phrase feedback carefully and to notice withdrawal behaviours early.

In workplaces, forward-thinking managers are drawing on the science to foster more inclusive environments. Some have introduced peer-awareness workshops that explain how rejection sensitivity can influence performance reviews, collaboration, and morale. The framing is not about singling people out, but about raising collective awareness of how small acts of clarity and encouragement improve everyone's sense of belonging.

The Role of Advocacy and Patient Voices

Research has also amplified advocacy. Online forums and support groups often share study summaries, encouraging members to bring them into medical appointments. Patients armed with citations about brain imaging or assessment tools find they are taken more seriously by clinicians. This dynamic flips the old power balance: lived experience now pushes research forward, while research in turn validates lived experience.

The Road Ahead

Toward Formal Recognition

One of the key milestones still ahead is formal recognition in diagnostic systems. Many clinicians argue that even if RSD does not become a stand-alone diagnosis, it deserves a defined status as a specifier within ADHD or related conditions. Recognition at this level would drive insurance coverage for therapy, fund larger research studies, and signal to patients that their experiences are legitimate.

Expanding Treatment Options

Medication research is still in its early stages, but clinical trials are expected to broaden in the next decade. If existing medications can be fine-tuned for emotional regulation, or if new compounds emerge, patients will have more evidence-based options. The same applies to psychotherapy: the next step is developing structured, manualised interventions specifically for rejection sensitivity, which can then be tested in rigorous trials.

Embedding Cross-Disciplinary Knowledge

The most hopeful future is one where RSD is not siloed in psychiatry alone. Collaboration with educators, workplace leaders, and digital health innovators could transform prevention and care. If rejection sensitivity is recognised as a biopsychosocial issue, not just an individual burden, then entire systems can be reshaped to reduce harm and promote resilience.

The Role of Global Communities

Online communities have already been instrumental in driving awareness. The future likely holds even greater partnerships between patient voices and researchers. Co-designing studies with people who live with RSD every day ensures that the right questions are asked. It also means that results are more likely to be relevant and accessible.

Closing Reflections

Hope in the context of RSD does not mean pretending the pain is small. It means recognising that pain and still seeing the progress around it. Twenty years ago, people lived with rejection sensitivity in silence, with no name and little understanding. Today, the language exists. Researchers are investigating its roots. Clinicians are adapting their practices. Patients are finding each other and telling their stories without shame.

The science is young, but it is moving. Each paper, each trial, and each conversation shifts the landscape from confusion toward clarity. And while definitive cures may not yet exist, the trajectory points toward more recognition, more tools, and more compassion in the years ahead.

For those living with RSD, this is not abstract. It means the possibility of therapy that speaks directly to their struggles. It means medication trials that may ease the sharpness of rejection. It means being met by teachers, managers, or partners who have read the same studies and now understand.

Above all, it means hope that the next generation will not grow up believing they are weak for feeling deeply. Instead, they will know their brains respond differently, and that difference can be met with wisdom rather than dismissal.

Chap 21: A Life Not Defined by RSD

Choosing a Broader Identity

When people first discover RSD, the relief is immense. At last, there is a name for the unbearable intensity of rejection and criticism. But there is also a risk: that the label becomes the whole story of who they are. While RSD may explain patterns, it does not define a person's worth or destiny. This chapter is about reclaiming identity beyond the condition.

Beyond Labels

Psychological labels can be double-edged. They clarify, but they can also confine. Someone who hears, "You have rejection sensitivity," may think, "That's why my relationships fail" or "That's why I can't succeed at work." Such thoughts can spiral into resignation. Yet the same label, reframed, can empower: "This is why my emotions feel intense. And this is where I can make choices that fit me."

Defining oneself only through RSD is like defining a forest only by its storms. The storms are real, but they are not the whole ecosystem. The forest is also full of growth, shelter, and resilience. Identity must be built around the full picture.

Reclaiming Strengths

One way forward is to recognise the strengths that come with sensitivity. People with RSD often have acute empathy, strong intuition about others' feelings, and a capacity for deep loyalty in relationships. These qualities are not incidental; they are often two sides of the same coin as rejection sensitivity. What wounds in one setting can nurture in another.

For example, a person who feels devastated by exclusion may also be the friend who notices when others are left out. The pain they know equips them to create inclusion for others. That is not "making the best of it." It is reframing sensitivity as a power that has value in the world.

The Role of Narrative

Our identities are shaped by the stories we tell ourselves. For years, someone with RSD may have carried a story of failure, embarrassment, or shame. But stories are not fixed; they can be rewritten. When therapy, research, or lived experience gives someone new language, they can start telling themselves a different story: not "I am broken," but "I am human, and my sensitivity has meaning."

Narratives matter because they shape behaviour. A person who sees themselves as doomed will withdraw. A person who sees themselves as resilient will step forward. Both can be true of the same person; the story chosen makes the difference.

Building Multiple Roles

Another way to prevent RSD from dominating identity is to cultivate multiple roles in life. A person may be a partner, parent, athlete, volunteer, or artist. When one role is shaken by rejection, others remain as anchors. This diversification of self reduces the risk that every setback feels catastrophic.

Even small roles matter. Joining a community choir, mentoring a younger colleague, or volunteering locally adds threads to the fabric of identity. The richer the fabric, the harder it is for one tear to unravel it all.

Accepting, Not Resisting

Many people approach RSD as if it is a flaw to be erased. They spend years trying to harden themselves against rejection, believing that if they can just toughen up enough, they will finally stop feeling so raw. This pursuit often leads to exhaustion. The reality is that rejection sensitivity cannot be switched off by sheer willpower. It is part of how the nervous system processes threat.

Acceptance, in this context, is liberating. Accepting does not mean giving up. It means saying, "I may always feel these surges, but I can decide how to respond." For example, instead of collapsing into self-blame after a colleague's sharp tone, a person might pause, recognise the surge as RSD, and take a walk before responding. The pain remains, but it no longer dictates every action.

Some find it useful to give RSD a nickname, a way of externalising it. "That's my storm voice talking," one person told me. By naming it, they were able to remind themselves: "The storm is passing. I do not have to mistake it for the truth."

Choosing Where to Invest Energy

Sensitivity can make all slights feel equally significant. A stranger's dismissive glance may sting as sharply as a close friend's criticism. But living beyond RSD involves learning to triage experiences: not every wound deserves equal attention.

Consider two scenarios. In one, a barista forgets your order and looks irritated when you remind them. In another, a trusted friend cancels plans without explanation. Both might trigger the familiar RSD spiral. Yet only one, the friend, has long-term significance. Recognising this distinction allows a person to protect their emotional reserves.

Therapists often use scaling techniques to build this skill. Clients are asked: "On a scale from one to ten, how important is this person in your life? How much will this matter in six months?" Over time, this practice becomes instinctive, helping people conserve energy for the connections that truly matter.

Anchoring in Values

Values are a stabiliser in the storm of sensitivity. When rejection threatens to unmoor identity, values can hold someone steady. For instance, someone whose core value is compassion can remind themselves: "Even if I feel unwanted right now, I can still live out compassion today."

Anchoring in values transforms pain into direction. A student who fails an exam may feel deep rejection, interpreting it as proof of being "stupid" or "incapable." But if their value is learning, they can reframe the setback: "This hurts, but my value is to keep growing." The pain does not disappear, but it no longer dictates identity.

Values-based living is a central theme in Acceptance and Commitment Therapy (ACT), and it resonates strongly for those with RSD. By tying behaviour to values rather than fear of rejection, people shift from defensive to purposeful living.

Practising Self-Compassion

The harsh inner critic is often the loudest voice in RSD. After even small slights, the mind may replay mistakes, calling the person "stupid," "boring," or "unlovable." Self-compassion interrupts this pattern.

Practical self-compassion exercises include:

- The supportive friend test: What would you say to a friend in your shoes? Can you extend that kindness inward?
- Common humanity reminders: Telling oneself, "Everyone makes mistakes. Rejection is part of being human."
- Soothing rituals: Placing a hand on the chest, breathing deeply, and repeating a compassionate phrase such as, "This is painful, but I am safe."

Research consistently shows that self-compassion reduces anxiety, lowers stress hormones, and builds resilience. For someone with RSD, self-compassion is not indulgence. It is medicine.

Protecting Joy

RSD narrows focus to what hurts. Joy expands focus back to what nourishes. Protecting joy means deliberately making space for activities, people, and places that bring lightness.

This may involve creative hobbies, nature walks, music, or humour. Importantly, joy should not be treated as optional. It is protective. People with RSD who actively schedule joyful experiences report fewer spirals and faster recovery when rejection strikes.

Even small joys matter. Watching a favourite sitcom, sharing a meal with a safe friend, or playing with a pet creates moments that counterbalance pain. These moments build a memory bank of warmth that rejection cannot fully erase.

The Power of Relationships and Community

Why Connection Matters

RSD thrives in isolation. Alone, the mind has free rein to replay slights, magnify criticism, and spin rejection into catastrophe. Relationships provide counterweight. A supportive friend or group can reflect back a more accurate picture: "You are valued here." That reflection does not erase the pain of rejection, but it softens its grip.

Humans are wired for connection. Social bonds have been shown in countless studies to buffer stress, strengthen immunity, and extend lifespan. For those with RSD, the stakes are even higher. Connection is not just comforting. It is protective against the cycles of withdrawal and self-condemnation that rejection sensitivity can trigger.

Choosing Safe People

Not all relationships nourish. Some people thrive on competition, sarcasm, or criticism, and these dynamics can amplify RSD. Part of living beyond the condition is learning to choose safe people: those who respect boundaries, offer consistency, and treat sensitivity with dignity.

Safe people are not flawless. They may still make mistakes, but their pattern is one of care. One sign of safety is repair: if they hurt you, they come back to make it right. Building life around such people reduces the emotional whiplash that RSD often magnifies.

The Role of Peer Support

Peer groups, both in-person and online, can be transformative. There is unique relief in hearing someone else describe the same spirals you thought were yours alone. Online forums and support circles provide this mirror. The danger is that some groups spiral into negativity, but well-moderated spaces can be a lifeline.

Sharing stories of rejection and recovery normalises the experience. It allows people to move from "I am broken" to "I am part of a community that understands." That shift is profound. It redefines identity from solitary suffering to shared humanity.

Intimacy and Belonging

For many with RSD, the deepest fear is abandonment. Yet intimacy, the very closeness that feels dangerous, is also the most healing. Safe, steady relationships allow a person to test vulnerability and discover that not every slip leads to rejection.

This does not happen overnight. It unfolds in gradual steps: sharing a small fear, revealing a personal story, expressing an opinion. Each time the relationship holds, the internal belief that "I am unlovable" weakens. Over months and years, intimacy becomes not a threat but a resource.

Community as Identity Anchor

When identity is anchored only in the self, rejection can feel shattering. But when identity is anchored in community, no single rejection has the power to define worth. Whether through a religious group, a creative collective, a volunteer team, or a local club, belonging expands the frame of identity.

Community says: "You are more than your latest mistake." It provides continuity. It says: "You belong here, even when you falter." For people with RSD, this is not abstract. It is a daily antidote to the belief that rejection makes them disposable.

Living Forward with Purpose

Shaping a Future Narrative

A life not defined by RSD is one where the condition is acknowledged but not central. This begins with narrative choice: asking not "What has rejection taken from me?" but "What direction do I want to grow toward?" Reframing the question shifts energy from defending against pain to pursuing meaning.

Building Resilience Through Growth

Growth emerges when challenges are not avoided but integrated. A person who once avoided relationships for fear of rejection might instead set a goal of building one trustworthy friendship. Each step toward that goal strengthens resilience. This resilience is not the absence of sensitivity, but the ability to keep moving even when sensitivity flares.

Aligning with Passions

Purpose grows when passions are pursued without apology. Many with RSD have talents in creativity, caregiving, or problem-solving precisely because of their sensitivity. Leaning into these passions transforms the narrative from "I am too sensitive" to "My sensitivity fuels what I love."

For example, an artist who channels rejection pain into painting is not defined by RSD. They are defined by artistry. A mentor who uses their empathy to support younger colleagues is not ruled by sensitivity. They are remembered for generosity.

Leaving Space for Joy and Play

Purpose is not always heavy. It includes joy, humour, and play. Building a life not defined by RSD means deliberately leaving room for lightness. This protects against the risk of defining life only by survival. Thriving requires space for laughter, curiosity, and delight.

Closing Reflections

Living with RSD can feel like carrying a shadow that stretches across every corner of life. But shadows only exist where there is light. A life not defined by RSD is one that turns deliberately toward that light; identity, values, relationships, and passions that reach far beyond rejection.

This does not mean the pain disappears. It means the pain is no longer the narrator of the story. The person is.

When people accept sensitivity as part of their wiring, when they anchor identity in community and values, when they cultivate joy alongside resilience, they step into a broader life. RSD becomes one chapter in a much larger book, not the title on the cover.

The ultimate goal is not to deny the reality of RSD, nor to romanticise it. The goal is balance: a recognition that sensitivity shapes experience, but does not determine destiny.

And perhaps most importantly: living beyond RSD does not happen alone. It is sustained by safe people, meaningful roles, and communities that remind us who we are when shame tries to tell us otherwise. That is not just hope. It is the lived reality of many who now know; they are more than their pain.

That's living, laughing and loving.

FAQ

A

ADHD: Is RSD always part of ADHD?

No. While rejection sensitivity is very common in ADHD, it can also appear in people without ADHD. The overlap is strong, but not absolute. Clinicians often describe RSD as one of the most impairing aspects of ADHD, yet research shows that people with autism, anxiety, or trauma histories may also experience it.

Anger: Why does RSD sometimes look like sudden rage?

For some, rejection triggers not just sadness but intense anger. This is often a defensive response — anger shields against the shame of feeling unwanted. It does not mean the person is violent or unsafe, but it can strain relationships if unaddressed. Learning to pause, name the surge, and step back before responding helps reduce harm.

B

Biology: Is RSD "all in my head"?

Yes and no. It is in the brain, but that does not mean it is imaginary. Brain scans show that the same regions activated by physical pain are also activated during rejection. Neurochemicals like dopamine and norepinephrine play roles. In other words, RSD is biological as well as emotional.

Breakups: Why do they feel unbearable with RSD?

Because RSD magnifies rejection, the loss of a relationship can feel like identity collapse. The pain is real, not weakness. Support, therapy, and safe community can soften the impact. Over time, people do heal — though the process may be slower and more intense than for others.

C

Children: Can kids have RSD?

Yes. Many children show signs of extreme sensitivity to criticism, exclusion, or even mild disapproval. They may cry easily, withdraw, or lash out when they feel unwanted. Supporting children involves clear reassurance, predictable routines, and teaching gentle coping skills early.

Criticism: Why does even mild feedback feel devastating?

RSD hijacks the brain's threat system. A simple comment like "You missed a comma" can be experienced as "You are incompetent." The intensity comes from how the nervous system interprets threat, not from a lack of resilience.

D

Diagnosis: Is there an official test for RSD?

No. There is no entry for RSD in diagnostic manuals. Some questionnaires measure rejection sensitivity, but they are research tools, not diagnostic instruments. Diagnosis is usually clinical, based on patterns of lived experience.

Disability: Can RSD be considered a disability?

In some cases, yes. If the symptoms are severe enough to impair work, education, or daily functioning, accommodations may be available under disability law. This varies by country and depends on whether RSD is linked to ADHD, autism, or another recognised condition.

E

Employment: How can I manage RSD at work?

Clarity is key. Ask managers for feedback that is specific and balanced, not vague. Create rituals to ground yourself after meetings. If disclosure feels safe, explaining RSD to a trusted colleague or supervisor can reduce misunderstandings.

Exclusion: Why does being left out hurt so much?

Humans are wired to seek belonging. For people with RSD, exclusion activates the same brain pathways as physical pain. The intensity is not weakness. It is biology. Knowing this helps shift self-blame toward self-understanding.

F

Family: How can families best support someone with RSD?

By offering consistency, reassurance, and patience. Avoiding sarcasm and casual cruelty makes a big difference. Families can also help by encouraging therapy, celebrating strengths, and reminding the person that their value is not tied to perfection.

Friends: What role do friends play in recovery?

A vital one. Friends provide mirrors that challenge shame-driven narratives. Safe, steady friendships remind people with RSD that they are valued beyond their fears. Even one supportive friend can dramatically change the course of healing.

G

Genetics: Is RSD inherited?

Research suggests a genetic component, particularly in overlap with ADHD. Twin studies indicate that heightened rejection sensitivity runs in families. Genetics is not destiny, but it does increase vulnerability, especially when combined with environmental stress.

Grief: How does RSD affect grieving?

Grief is already painful, but RSD can intensify feelings of abandonment. Someone may interpret a loved one's death as a kind of rejection, even though they know logically it was not. Supportive counselling helps untangle grief from rejection sensitivity.

H

Hope: Can RSD improve over time?

Yes. With therapy, medication in some cases, and supportive relationships, many people find the intensity of RSD lessens. They still feel sensitive, but they recover faster and interpret situations more accurately. Improvement is possible.

Humour: Is joking about RSD harmful or helpful?

It depends. Self-aware humour can provide relief and perspective. But cruel jokes from others often wound deeply. Safe humour acknowledges sensitivity without belittling it.

I

Identity: Will RSD always define me?

No. RSD may shape some experiences, but it does not define a person's whole identity. By cultivating values, roles, and relationships, people can live lives where RSD is a feature, not the headline.

Isolation: Why do I isolate myself after feeling rejected?

Isolation is a self-protective reflex. Withdrawing feels safer than risking more hurt. The challenge is that isolation often deepens shame. Gentle reconnection, even in small steps, helps break the cycle.

J

Jealousy: Is jealousy part of RSD?

It can be. People with RSD may compare themselves constantly, fearing rejection if they do not measure up. Jealousy in this context is less about envy and more about fear of being replaced or excluded.

Jobs: Should I tell my employer about RSD?

Disclosure is a personal choice. Some find it helpful to explain sensitivity in general terms, asking for clear feedback and predictability. Others prefer to keep it private, using coping strategies quietly. The decision depends on workplace culture and trust.

K

Kids: How can I tell if my child has RSD?

Look for patterns: extreme distress at mild criticism, explosive reactions to feeling left out, or constant reassurance-seeking. These signs do not guarantee RSD, but they suggest heightened sensitivity. A professional evaluation can clarify.

Kindness: Does kindness really help?

Yes. Small acts of kindness - a thoughtful message, a patient explanation, a gentle tone - can mean the world to someone with RSD. Kindness does not cure the condition, but it softens its sharp edges.

L

Labels: Should I even use the term RSD?

Labels are tools. For some, the term RSD brings validation and clarity. For others, it feels limiting. Use the language that empowers you. The important thing is understanding the pattern and finding strategies that help.

Love: How does RSD affect romantic relationships?

It can make them both intense and fragile. Fear of abandonment may cause clinginess or withdrawal. Yet the same sensitivity can bring deep empathy and loyalty. With open communication and patient partners, many people with RSD build fulfilling relationships.

M

Medication: Does medication work for RSD?

There is no pill designed specifically for RSD. Some clinicians prescribe medications that target emotional regulation, such as stimulants, alpha-2 agonists, or certain antidepressants. Results vary. Medication is best combined with therapy and lifestyle support.

Mindfulness: Can mindfulness help?

Yes. Mindfulness teaches people to observe their reactions without being consumed by them. Regular practice helps create a pause between trigger and response, reducing the spiral that RSD can set off.

N

Neurodivergence: Is RSD only found in neurodivergent people?

No. While RSD is common in ADHD and autism, it is not exclusive to them. Some people without formal neurodivergent conditions also experience extreme rejection sensitivity. However, the overlap is strong enough that many researchers view RSD as part of the broader neurodivergent experience.

Normality: Does everyone feel rejection this strongly?

No. Everyone dislikes rejection, but in RSD the intensity is disproportionate. What others might brush off in an hour can haunt someone with RSD for days or weeks. This difference in intensity is what makes it distinct.

O

Overreaction: Why do people accuse me of overreacting?

Because from the outside, the depth of pain is not always visible. Others may see only the tears, anger, or withdrawal, not the neurological surge driving it. The response feels "too much" to them, but it is appropriate to the inner experience. Explaining this difference can help.

Optimism: Is optimism possible with RSD?

Yes. Optimism is not denial of pain, but a focus on possibility. People with RSD often develop a unique form of optimism: cautious, grounded, and deeply appreciative of safe relationships. Hope grows stronger when supported by therapy, community, and progress in research.

P

Parents: How can parents balance discipline with RSD?

By being firm but gentle. Children with RSD still need boundaries, but harsh criticism often backfires. Parents can frame discipline as guidance: "I know you're capable of doing this differently," rather than "You failed again." Balance is key - structure plus reassurance.

Perfectionism: Is perfectionism linked to RSD?

Very often. Fear of criticism pushes many people with RSD to chase flawlessness. While this can lead to achievements, it is exhausting. Learning to tolerate mistakes as part of growth is essential to breaking the perfectionism–rejection cycle.

Q

Questions: What questions should I ask a therapist about RSD?

- Do you have experience with rejection sensitivity?
- How would you adapt therapy for my triggers?
- What strategies can I practise between sessions?

Asking direct questions ensures therapy is tailored, not generic.

Quitting: Why do I quit projects when I fear rejection?

Because anticipation of rejection can feel as painful as rejection itself. Many people with RSD pre-emptively abandon projects to avoid potential shame. Recognising this pattern is the first step to interrupting it. Setting smaller goals and tolerating imperfect outcomes can help.

R

Relationships: Can RSD ruin relationships?

It can strain them, yes. Misinterpretations and withdrawal may create distance. But with awareness and support, many relationships survive and even thrive. Clear communication and safe repair processes are crucial.

Resilience: Can someone with RSD become resilient?

Yes. Resilience is not the absence of pain, but the ability to recover from it. People with RSD who practise self-compassion, anchor in values, and build safe communities often develop profound resilience. Their sensitivity becomes a strength when paired with coping tools.

S

School: How does RSD affect students?

Students with RSD may fear answering questions, avoid group work, or melt down after criticism. Teachers who give feedback gently and celebrate effort as much as results can make school far less threatening.

Shame: Why is shame so strong in RSD?

Because rejection threatens identity. Shame is the emotion that says, "I am unworthy." For people with RSD, even small slights can trigger that core wound. Addressing shame through therapy, compassion, and community is central to healing.

Support: What kind of support works best?

Support that is consistent, patient, and non-judgmental. Friends, family, and partners who offer clear reassurance without condescension are especially helpful. Professional support from therapists who understand RSD adds another layer of stability.

T

Teachers: How can teachers support students with RSD?

By giving feedback privately when possible, framing criticism as guidance, and celebrating progress as much as results. Predictable routines and encouragement help students feel secure enough to risk mistakes.

Therapy: What type of therapy works best for RSD?

No single therapy has been proven superior, but cognitive behavioural therapy, compassion-focused therapy, and Acceptance and Commitment Therapy (ACT) are often adapted successfully. The most important factor is a therapist who understands rejection sensitivity and tailors strategies to it.

U

Understanding: How can I help others understand RSD?

Explain that rejection activates the same brain regions as physical pain. Share that the reaction is not weakness but biology. Concrete examples - like how a missed text feels like abandonment - often help others grasp the reality.

Unpredictability: Why do small triggers sometimes feel huge?

Because the nervous system does not always scale reactions logically. A minor slight can activate the same circuits as a major rejection. The intensity reflects brain wiring, not the importance of the event itself.

V

Validation: Why does validation help so much?

Validation tells the person their experience is real and understood. It does not require agreement, only acknowledgment: "I see that this hurt you." Validation soothes the shame that fuels RSD.

Vulnerability: Is it safe to be vulnerable if I have RSD?

Vulnerability feels dangerous, but it is also healing. Sharing fears with safe people allows new experiences of acceptance, which slowly overwrite the expectation of rejection.

W

Workplace: How can workplaces adapt for RSD?

By promoting clear, constructive feedback; offering private channels for correction; and fostering inclusive environments. Workplaces that prioritise clarity and kindness benefit everyone, not just those with RSD.

Worth: How do I stop tying my worth to others' opinions?

It takes practice. Anchoring identity in values, cultivating multiple roles, and practising self-compassion help shift self-worth from external validation to internal stability.

X

X-factor: Can RSD ever be a strength?

Yes. Sensitivity can fuel empathy, creativity, and loyalty. Many people with RSD notice subtleties others miss and use that insight to build deep, meaningful connections.

Y

Youth: Is RSD different in young people?

Yes. In children and teens, RSD often shows up as explosive outbursts, avoidance of school, or intense withdrawal. Early recognition and support can prevent these patterns from hardening into adult shame.

Yes/no questions: Why do I dread them?

Because even simple yes/no questions can feel loaded with the possibility of rejection. The fear is not about the question itself, but about what the answer might imply for belonging.

Z

Zero tolerance: Should I cut off everyone who triggers my RSD?

Not necessarily. Some relationships are toxic and may need boundaries or distance. But if every trigger leads to cutting ties, isolation follows. The goal is balance: knowing when to set limits, and when to repair and continue.

www.ingramcontent.com/pod-product-compliance
Lightning Source LLC
LaVergne TN
LVHW052313200926
848481LV00002B/554
* 9 7 8 1 0 6 7 0 6 8 2 3 3 *